The anonymous author of this volume was for many years an active member of a witches' coven. He participated in witchcraft ceremonies and witnessed all the innermost secrets of the Craft. When he left he took with him his book of witches' rules – a document so secret that even those in the Craft are not allowed to see it all at once. The author's courageous decision to publish this guide and text to the sacred ceremonies of witchcraft has already placed him under pain of death.

The Devil's Prayerbook

A Witch

Mayflower

Granada Publishing Limited
Published in 1975 by Mayflower Books Ltd
Frogmore, St Albans, Herts AL2 2NF

First published in Great Britain by
Rigel Press Ltd 1972

Made and printed in Great Britain by
Hazell Watson & Viney Ltd
Aylesbury, Bucks
Set in Linotype Times

CONTENTS

INTRODUCTION

Modern witchcraft is based on an assortment of theories, superstitions, ignorance, some black magic, and, occasionally, some very questionable practices.

Coven leaders hold on to their followers using awe and apprehension. Should the follower desire to leave the coven, fear of 'occult reprisal' is used. This is a difficult fear to remove and some coven leaders have much psychological distress to answer for – their 'witchcraft' is both dangerous and harmful.

The original concept of witchcraft is one of nature and plant lore. It required considerable experience to handle many of the recipes associated with the Witches. Many plants are poisonous and some of the traditional mixtures are bizarre but in ancient times plants were virtually the only medicines available, and witch-knowledge was not for the idle meddler.

The wise ones of old had little in common with the modern witch of today. They were frequently solitary workers who could not take long journeys each month at full moon to celebrate rites to the Goddess or the Horned God. The idea of a nude witch is not traditional to this country, it is an idea imported from a warmer climate; though in some covens today it is exploited entirely for its sexual undertones.

The English climate is not conducive to naked rompings in the dark, even in the warmest days of summer. Moreover, in all the surviving records of our witchcraft trials, nobody was ever accused of working naked – surely it would have been noted if they had.

Witches dancing a magic circle is a traditional picture, but the idea of a witch performing a traditional ritual is not true. The practices were never written down in ancient days, partly for reasons of secrecy and partly because very few people could read or write. Ceremonial magic requires exact working to a given formula, but many witch covens have their own formulae. Today members of the coven write down their traditions in a 'Book of Shadows'. Many rituals enacted by the coven I was with were strictly Ceremonial Magic and, in most cases, poorly done or rehearsed. This is ignorance in the extreme and very dangerous.

Some of the practices which appear in this 'Book of Shadows' are questionable. The ritual scourging is not native to this country and derives from the Christian sect, the Flagellates, of the Middle Ages. Today it is often used to cover a wild indulgence in flagellation. The scourge with its eight thongs and five knots in each tail, when used as a punishment tool, usually called for by the High Priestess for some misdemeanour, can be very painful. The coven claimed that use of a scourge made the blood move faster to encourage the raising of power. That was not all that it raised. The sight of an elderly man flogging a naked, kneeling, bound young woman is sexually stimulating and so is the reverse with its implication of sexual domination and submission.

The presentation of the working tools, especially the athame, and the white handled knife, is another example of sexual involvement. It is done by pressing the tools against the breasts of a woman who then presses herself against the man. On more than one occasion this gave rise to sexual excitement. Indeed, once the five-fold salute was given in such a way that it was unmistakably cunnilingus and fellatio, nor was there any attempt to stop this – indeed, everybody seemed to think it was amusing. However, later the same evening the couple were privately interviewed, and, as a result of the censure, they left shortly after to set up their own group. This particular event occurred when rivalry between covens had reached a new height and the amount of sheer bitchiness was incredible. From time to time this situation arises and can only be likened to petulant children claiming incredible abilities for their own gangs. After a few months feelers would be put out and eventually all would be friends again.

The Great Rite, or Third Degree, because of its sexual involvement, is frequently abused. It can certainly be harmful, or downright dangerous. There are many variations on the Sex-in-Magic theme but it is supposed that, at the moment of orgasm, the psychic senses and abilities of the individual can be heightened. Experiments in prolonging these moments are legion – and not just in magic. This is fine if the male and female can be matched with some sort of equality but ages in coven members fall between eighteen to the late fifties or more. The mating of an old man with a young girl, or a young man with an old woman is not always a delicate experiment, nor does it always take note of 'sympathetic fertility'. With the decision of the High Priestess as final in the selection of the celebrants, I am convinced that there has often been more than just the ritual in mind before the choice is made.

Then there is the physical side to be considered. The choice taken, coitus interruptus or the complete act, is left up to the celebrants. To the best of my belief, no one really knew what went on behind the locked doors but the excitement of those involved was always apparent. There were no virgins in the coven of which I was a member.

In Black Covens there would be witnessed sex, perhaps in group form but rumour is my guide and most covens do not go beyond the bounds of normal decency.

With all these activities going on, and the rumours that reach the outside world from time to time, covens get a lot of applications for membership. Applicants come from all walks of life, and they are people of all ages. All applications are considered but some are rejected because they are homosexuals, people with certain medical conditions, those who have no idea what the craft is about, or, those who are too young.

Plenty of sexual deviates apply but few get further than the first interview. Those with medical conditions are not allowed either – the excitement and activities are not conducive to long life with a bad heart or some other infirmity.

Those with little idea of what witchcraft is about usually write quite intelligent first letters but their initial interview reveals the lack of knowledge.

It is the young that give the most headaches. Because of the tremendous psychological and sexual involvement, the young should be discouraged from joining a coven but in many cases they are not. My own coven had an age limit of seventeen, and to give them credit, they held to it steadfastly. Other covens do not.

There are groups that snap up young people as they come along. Others lead them on until such time as they appreciate what is going on and have little chance to change their minds. In November 1971 at a meeting of people to question witches about the craft, I counted fifteen young people present. Most of their questions were serious but the answers invited more interest, and an open invitation to come and witness a ritual was accepted with alacrity.

From here there is only one step further to go and that is to join. To get out is difficult, the young do not realize how hard it can be. They are made welcome at a time when they cannot appreciate the moral and spiritual dangers involved but the same goes for many adults who join under the same circumstances. It's easy to get in and very, very difficult to get out.

The pressure put on members is outlined in some Initiation Ceremonies. Remember, they do not know what it is they are going in for, but they are impressed with the 'taking of their measure', the oath of allegiance, and that 'may weapons turn against them should they break this solemn, solemn oath.'

Very shortly after this, they are given a 'Book of Shadows' to copy out. In the chapter on Obedience it is stressed that you never question the demands made on you.

All this, within the first few weeks, will impress the suggestible neophyte with an aura of mystery, strange powers, and the ability of senior coven members to inflict terrible vengeance on them. As time goes on, these feelings grow, especially when the neophyte begins to doubt some of the practices. The first suggestion to the High Priestess that you wish to rethink the whole idea is often met with a kindly talk over a cup of tea; rather like a naughty child being tolerantly but firmly held to its obligations. From this point the member is watched, just to see how the land lies. Possibly a 'banishing ritual' is performed because this has an electrifying effect on wavering members. Ritual curses and invocations to gods to strike one down imply all manner of terrifying penalties. A departing member is carefully reminded of this consequence, and it shuts them up as a rule.

The waverers left behind are confused with conflicting beliefs and emotions, lost and terrified as to the correct thing to do. They are trapped by their own beliefs which bring on neurosis and panic. No one can lift this depression, save, perhaps, by a form of exorcism, or by proving conclusively that there is nothing to be afraid of.

The attempts to retrieve my copy of 'The Book of Shadows' were many and ingenious. Information was relayed that the Banishing Ritual was performed, together with all sorts of threats and curses to bring me to heel.

I had left the coven because my academic interest in the Craft was suffering. Nothing happened to prove that there was any special power inherent in the Craft or its followers. At the time there was a lot of trouble in the movement generally, and the press were having a field day. I left the coven for good, along with a couple of others. I believe one of these, a young girl, was 'reclaimed' and experienced a little trouble. She is still a reluctant member of the group.

Yet another feature with a strong element of danger is the use of aromatics, drugs, decoctions and ointments in some covens. Providing these are used under carefully controlled conditions, there can be little harm in their application, but they are seldom so controlled.

Decoctions of various plants to aid certain abilities are frequently employed without fully understanding their use. Sometimes there is a fully qualified practitioner on hand to give advice but many covens experiment without proper preparation, and without materials to hand for first aid, when necessary. For example, Patchouli correctly applied can aid psychotic tendencies and meditation. Taken internally, it is highly dangerous.

The foxglove gives digitalis, the poppy, opium – both are dangerous if used wrongly. What if Vervain or any other plant or herb is used indiscriminately? Perfumes and incenses are used to create atmosphere but they can give hallucinatory effects. The idea behind their usage is to separate the mind and body from everyday noises and influences to concentrate on the magic in hand. Few covens have a witch who can render first aid. I was present when one coven member fainted but fortunately qualified help was on hand that evening. What happens when no help is available?

Analysis of the psychological side is less easy. It sometimes involves a form of self-blackmail and the results are most difficult to erase from a troubled mind. We all suffer terrors and fears which have no obvious origin, even though others possess the same feelings. It may be a dislike of the dark, fear of cobwebs and spiders and so on. Spilled salt, crossed knives, open umbrellas or walking under ladders are very common superstitions supposed to bring bad luck. Frequently there are no logical explanations for obsessions, though curses can be and are effective.

For those who suffer the fear of a vengeful witch, the

emotion increases a hundredfold. If the victim has a little knowledge, this can be a very dangerous thing, for it creates all kinds of terrors. The knowledge of evil is recognized but the fear of the witch and the coven becomes so deep that nothing can remove it.

The correct treatment by experts takes a long time. The full implication of what magic and witchcraft are can disturb the psyche and even lead to insanity. The physical body suffers during the mental conflict for peace of mind.

No words of mine will fully describe the situation in the way it deserves, nor will it allay the fears of those who are beginning to undergo this long torture.

What I can say to those people – and those who want to experiment in witchcraft – is: Do not go further than reading about it. These 'witches' have little power but by these acts they do inflict heartache and misery on those in their clutches.

Consider a few facts that have hitherto been taken for granted.

Neophytes are told that the secrets of witches may never be revealed. Why, then, do witches permit those little excursions of writers and the press into their covens? Why do they give away snippets here and there to titillate the credulous? Why do they allow parts of their 'Book of Shadows' to be published? Why do they show some of the rituals on television and appear to explain the meaning behind some of their activities? What punishments are meted out to the press, the interviewer or the betrayer? (Punishment, remember, is contradictory with the requirements of the craft.)

Nothing.

Why, then, should the rank and file craft member be 'leaned upon', not to do as they themselves are doing?

When dealing with witches much goes unexplained and unanswered. It is expected that orders will be followed blindly as regrettably they often are. Now, perhaps, the witches can be fought on their own ground. Take away the veneer of secrecy and show the sort of practice that goes on, and witches will have little to use as a hold over the weak and foolish people they are now exploiting.

This 'Book of Shadows' was claimed to be a collection of writings handed down for many years. Some may detect the true origin, for it gives the impression of being far more recent.

It has never been published before in this form, as copied from a master copy by a coven member, although recently large chunks of it are to be found, differing slightly in wording, in several of the new books on the Craft.

To my mind it was simply a matter of time before a complete 'Book of Shadows' was put before the general public, perhaps by a sympathizer with the Craft. It must be evident that I am not a sympathizer. I have written this book by request to help those caught up in their web of fear. In my opinion the witch is unimaginative, a being with no power, no mystery and no magic.

It is all a grand delusion.

PART ONE

CHAPTER ONE

A Brief Outline of the Modern Witch

The modern witch follows the old religion of the Wicca, a faith of sympathetic magic and fertility that is dominated by the female. The male witch, or warlock, is of little importance to the coven.

Primarily it is the Goddess of the Moon who is the focal point of worship, and, to a lesser extent, the Horned God.

Witchcraft, the Way of the Wise, has nothing to do with Ceremonial Magic or Black Magic. It does have its own rites and rituals though in these you will find none of the reported sacrifices, sexual deviations or 'Black cocks and white hens being destroyed and their blood being poured over the body of a naked woman' (the last-mentioned being a voodoo spell).

Some witches work naked but this is entirely optional. Some covens use special robes. One witch, working out of doors, even uses consecrated gumboots; though most covens, who brave the vagaries of the English climate, make do with their members dressed alike in a plain white shift.

The normal coven consists of thirteen people when holding a ceremony, although there may be twenty or thirty people who belong to the coven. With today's requirements in business, etc., it is not always possible to attend the Monthly Meetings or the Festivals throughout the year. Some covens celebrate their meetings at full moon and some at new moon but usually meetings take place on the nearest Saturday night when the moon is waxing, never waning.

Extra to the thirteen meetings, or inclusive, are the following celebrations from January to December:

January – New or Full of the Moon
February – Candlemas, New or Full of the Moon
March – Vernal Equinox and New or Full of the Moon
April – Walpurgis Night and New or Full Moon
May – New or Full Moon
June – Midsummer Eve, Summer solstice meeting
July – New or Full of the Moon
August – Lammas or New or Full of the Moon
September – Autumn Equinox or New or Full of the Moon
October – Hallowe'en
November – New or Full of the Moon
December – Winter Solstice, New or Full of the Moon

These are the regular meeting nights of the year. Many covens meet every Saturday night to install neophytes or deal with requests from outsiders. Moreover, as it is their religion, they receive some pleasure from holding a religious meeting.

The Coven hierarchy is governed by the High Priestess and her deputy, the High Priest, the last named being having purely nominal powers. The High Priest usually interviews would-be initiates whilst the women deal with their own sex.

Also of prime importance in today's covens are the Astrologer, the Herbalist and the Teachers of the Craft. These would be members most adept in the sciences, the history of the Wicca and those well up on ritual invocation.

There are three degrees in witchcraft. The First Degree is the initiate, the newcomer. Some people never get beyond this level, it may be that they don't want to go further. This is permissible, for in the established church, not everyone takes up the priesthood, and in the Craft so long as they are content, no one questions the decision.

The Second Degree is that of the High Priestess or High Priest, these are the experienced people of the Craft, those who have trained to be the Astrologer or Herbalist,

Diviner or Lore Teacher. After twelve months they are raised to the higher degree and then, after further training, they begin instructing the new members. After attaining the Second Degree, they may even form their own coven. It is not permitted for a First Degree witch to form a coven, though in practice a High Priestess may allow an initiate to conduct a ceremony with promptings if they falter, much as a theatre prompter might do.

The ritual for attaining the Third Degree has never been written down in any Book of Shadows. It is deliberately omitted and rarely mentioned. When a Third Degree ritual is performed, no initiate or outsider is present. Generally the Third Degree is done at the New Moon and of course, away from the normal monthly meetings.

Occasionally other covens may be invited for the evening. Afterwards there is usually quite a celebration. Senior members may take the opportunity to develop policy to the outside world, plan a new coven or discuss research and achievement since the last meeting of such a nature.

Sometimes there is even a Grand Coven Meeting where all present are Third Degree Witches and therefore any rituals of magic performed should be exceptionally effective.

Third Degree Witchcraft is often referred to as the Great Rite, and, as the ritual is concerned with sex, it is here that wild stories of perversion and sexual debasement have their origin. There is little truth in these stories. The sexual part is optional but it may – and very often does – take place behind closed doors with nobody present except the celebrants.

Some further defence against these stories must be made. During any ordinary party as the evening wears on and the smoke hangs heavy in the air, couples pair off for petting, it's often the best part of the party. This may well take place after some Craft ceremonies; though there are no orgies in the more sincere circles. Some horseplay may occur but amusement is the prime mover, not sex.

Photographs are rarely taken. During my coven membership there were visits from the press and magazine photographers but no one blackmailed any prominent person in a compromising position. Even at a Witch wedding, the only sexual involvement was the five-fold kiss and a quick embrace with a token normal kiss.

The Craft and its members make a religion in spite of everything. The witches are frowned on by the Established Church, feared by the ignorant, despised by many and desired by the lustful. The Craft has a history of persecution but it survives by the loyalty of a few strong followers. Their zeal and fervour endure, despite the nasty stories.

Tales of young people being involved in witchcraft are mainly untrue. Young children belonging to coven members may be instructed in the craft or allowed to stay up for a bonfire but no one under eighteen is admitted to a Coven Night.

Interviewing would-be members for the coven is done in secrecy, not only for the sake of coven members but also for the sake of the aspirant. (With the publication of these rituals and with nothing held back, membership may even increase, once would-be witches know what they're in for!)

The sincere person will, if accepted by a good coven, be taught much. He, or she, will benefit from a deeper spiritual purpose and be the richer for it. The frivolous person and the dabbler should stay away, for the Way of the Wise is not for them.

CHAPTER TWO

Materials of the Craft

Like her forerunners, the modern witch uses mystic diagrams and tools, herbs, rare liquids and brews, incantations and rituals besides the religious aspect of Life. Today she also uses astrology and numerology. She seldom performs any of her activities outside a magic circle, for this is her protection if she makes a mistake. The circle can be permanently set up or it can be marked out at short notice.

A permanent circle exists in a sixteenth century Hertfordshire cottage. Inside is a circle and symbols, while the walls are covered with occult inscriptions – all mod cons laid on!

The witch will perform her ritual in perfect safety at the right time within the circle and usually the right time is during the hours of darkness. But to proceed, she must have the tools of the art which are mentioned in this 'Book of Shadows'.

These consist of the athame, a black handled knife with an inscribed hilt, and a matching white handled knife. Both must have been consecrated in a circle by a High Priestess before they can effectively be used. A witch will need a sword and several small dishes of silver, a candlestick for the altar and four other candlesticks to set at the cardinal points around the altar. Candles are very seldom black, in fact they are usually white, but some witches change the coloured candles to match the ritual. There should also be a small metal plate six inches across incribed with the pentagram of the circle.

Other tools are the wand, usually made of hazel and about fifteen inches long. There is also a scourge, the symbolic flail of the Egyptians, which has eight thongs about twelve inches long, each thong being knotted five times.

Several cords will be needed, red, white or silver, green or blue. Dressing gown cord is often used as it can be cut to the right length (4′ 6″) and comes ready coloured from many department stores.

Finally, small quantities of salt water and olive oil are needed to complete the scene.

Requirements vary from coven to coven. Some insist that women's personal jewellery should be placed on the altar before each ceremony and returned after consecration. Jewellery is aways silver for this is the metal of the moon and used for necklets, rings, earrings or armbands. Sometimes there is a single garter worn as a badge of office by the High Priestess. The garter may be black, though I have seen other colours used, the traditional material being snakeskin. Males generally wear no insignia of any sort, although some Third Degree men will wear a silver band on their upper arm.

Other materials needed during the ritual (cakes and wine, etc.) are placed behind the altar.

Although the circle once formed should not be broken, a 'gateway' is left to be opened and closed by the High Priestess as necessary. The gateway is usually between South and West.

The altar is usually set East to West, backing to North. It has to be big enough to take the tools of the art and it should be waist high. Technically the altar should never be round or oval but it does rather depend on the most useful table to hand. Sometimes the altar is placed in the centre of the group but in practice it is not always needed and it may be moved out of the way after the initial ceremony. Where a coven meets indoors, it is advisable to have a changing room and someone delegated to answer the door to unexpected visitors. Rituals should be worked by candlelight.

For an outdoor ceremony the altar is set in the North of the circle and the centre point of the working will be a small fire, enough to give off some heat but small enough for two people to leap over without danger. Clothes, or the lack of them, depend entirely on coven rules and weather.

A symbolic cauldron is used when rituals are held out of doors. This is traditionally used for the preparation of infusions and so on but it frequently serves as a soup kitchen or stew pot during a break in the ceremony.

Little statuettes of the Moon Goddess or the Horned God are often used as altar ornaments. The Goddess appears as Diana, most frequently cast in silver, although any metal except gold will do for her statue. The Horned God is frequently cast in bronze. You might even find appropriate statues in antique shops or junk stalls.

You usually find an incense burner at one corner of the altar. The incense symbolizes air in indoor ceremonies.

Some covens use joss sticks. If they're bought, they're usually the Chinese variety, not the Indian ones, but it is possible to make one's own, and incense can also be home-made, from traditional recipes.

Amulets, charms, talismans and so on are also made at home. Cakes are baked by a coven member and a bottle of vin blanc ordinaire is used for the Cakes and Wine ritual.

The size of the circle tends to vary from coven to coven. The original circle was 9′ in diameter and marked out using the 4′ 6″ cord. Today's circles are often 11′ in diameter with a 9′ circle inside. It's unnecessary to add mystic inscriptions between the circles, even if it looks terrific.

If you want to greet a witch, here's how it's done. The regular greeting is 'Blessed be' given with the sign of the Horned God. Contrary to popular belief, this is signalled by raising the little and fourth fingers as the thumb covers the folded index and third fingers.

Within the coven the five-fold salute is given by kissing the feet, knee, organs, breast and lips.

Scourging is also ritually symbolic as it is intended to

purge the soul with light strokes par derrière; a practice not limited to the Sabat but also practised by the penitents of Mother Church. Amongst the devout, the scourge was applied indiscriminately, but in a coven the prescribed number of forty strokes is applied in a peculiar sequence, 3 – 5 – 8 – 11 – 13, with a pause in the grouping.

Here are the directions for tying the cords ritually. The practitioner holds his right wrist with his left, behind his back. He is loosely bound with a cord that goes up round his neck and down again to make a triangle. Another cord is placed round the neck to be used as a halter or lead. A last cord is bound round the top of the left thigh – this mustn't trail on the ground, otherwise brethren might trip up and go flying.

Now we are almost ready. A length of red thread and a blindfold should complete the normal requirements but don't forget your small silver bell.

CHAPTER THREE

Planetary Hours and all That

The success of any magical ceremony depends on contacting the right surge of the time space continuum, hence today's witches consulting their Ephemeris before starting work. From now on please refer to any Old Moore's Almanac, that invaluable astral timetable. The time/tide tables of the unseen are divided into twenty-four hours – just wait till witchcraft reaches Mars!

These figures are based on the idea that planets can influence magical working and that the vibrations any planet emits are more dominant at certain times of the day or night than others. Philosophically this idea probably started in ancient Greece where people related deities to planets, i.e. the War God was Lord of the red planet Mars. This is very traditional.

One of the purposes of Magic as opposed to Witchcraft is to relate to specific areas of activity. These areas are summed up by the images associated with the Olympian gods – Saturn or Kronos represented Time and Form or Time and Space. Jupiter as king of the Gods was the Son of Time and represents the Laws which Space and Time impose. Mars is eruptive and often military energy. The Sun, half way between heaven and earth, was the source of Light and Life. Venus of the doves and leopards is savage and gentle simultaneously, as we see in nature and in ourselves. Mercury, the messenger of the Gods, is the communicating intelligence between ideal and form. The Moon with its interplay with Earth responding to the female tides, the sea tides, and the tides of life and death. If you want to practise magic, you'll have to know your way around the solar system!

Mother Shipton would have been less intellectual and

more concerned with the genii loci. She would appreciate that high noon in summer in a maternity ward would be the wrong place for necromancy, nor would the catacombs at midnight be exactly the right place for a ritual involving the Sun. Be that as it may, our Witches follow the Gregorian Calendar and its consequences with the equation

$$x = \frac{t - d}{12}$$

where x is the planetary hour, t is the twenty-four-hour cycle and d the period of daylight. The division sum would give you the length of the planetary hour at night. You can of course quite easily substitute n for d if you are interested in an hour of the day.

Working out the order of the planetary hours by day is very simple and I will not insult your intelligence by producing a long string of similar looking names. The thing to remember is this, each day starts with the planet from which it takes its name. Sunday – Sun, Monday – Moon, Tuesday – Mars, Wednesday – Mercury, Thursday – Jupiter, Friday – Venus, Saturday – Saturn. After that the planets govern the hours in the same order, e.g. Sunday; Sun, Venus, Mercury, Moon, Saturn, Jupiter, Mars, Sun, Venus, Mercury, Moon, Saturn, Jupiter, Mars, Sun, Venus, Mercury, Moon, Saturn. To pick the right planetary hour of the night you merely carry on so that the first hour of the night on Sunday would be referred to Jupiter, and then to Mars, Sun, Venus, Mercury, Moon, Saturn, Jupiter, Mars, Sun, Venus, Mercury.

If you know the Kabbalah you will recognize a pattern. If you're already a Mathematician, you might be able to explain how on this sequence, the first hour on any day always ends up as the planet referable to that day. And if you're not a Mathematician – there's a Ph.D in this for someone!

Obviously the length of the planetary hour by day or night will be affected by the orbit of the earth round the sun in summer or winter relative to the point of space in question on the earth. Without raising the question of what happens in the Land of the Midnight Sun, the planetary hours are obviously much longer or shorter at the solstices. Thus in Western Europe in December you most likely have a planetary hour one hour and twenty minutes long at night and correspondingly brief during the day. The importance of this is that some witches take the view that specific rituals should be worked within the framework of the appropriate planetary hour and must be designed accordingly.

Having sorted out the hours of the planets, you must know which planet can influence what – and the sun and the moon are regarded not only as planets but also as Individuality and Personality, Male and Female, etc.

THE SUN governs the following vocations: the theatre, T.V., radio, film producers, politicians, executives, financiers, directors, diplomats, 'the headers'. The jewels and metals are diamond, carbuncle, chrysolite, and so on, gold and topaz. Its animals are the lion, the eagle, the cock, the condor, the ibis and the parrot. The following plants are sacred to the sun, poppy, golden-rod, golden-glow, camomile, orrica, sunflower, scarlet sage, rose, peppermint, orange and tangerine plants, laurels, lavender, sage and thyme. The proper day for sun magic is Sunday and the night is Wednesday. The correct number is 1 and the colour is golden yellow.

THE MOON governs the following vocations: all aspects of the sea, impersonators, inns and hotels, Real Estate and the food industry. The jewels and metals are moonstone, pearl, emerald, beryl and silver, diamond crystal. The sacred animals include all shellfish, mosquitoes, bats, moths, rabbits and hares, nightingales, snails, frogs, cats, the goose and the swan. Plants governed by the moon are olive and willow trees, melons, pumpkins, narcissus, cabbage, watercress, cucumbers, water-rose, lily and lotus.

Moon magic is worked during the day of Monday or Thursday night. The colour is silver or white, and the number is 2 or 7.

MERCURY rules the publishing world, travel in all forms, commercial travellers and salesmen, the aircraft industry, medicine, scientists, street traders and so on. Jewels for this planet include carnelian, aquamarine, agate, mercury or quick-silver and aluminium. The sacred animals are the fox or vixen, the monkey, the lynx, insects of all kinds, spiders of all varieties, ants, the weasel (and the laughing hyena!). The plants are hazelnut, mulberry and ash trees, myrtle, clover and fern, burrs, celery, endives, madder, juniper, elder, parsley and thyme, caraway, spignel, arrowroot, lavender, lily-of-the-valley. The right day for Mercury magic is Wednesday and the night is Saturday. The number is 5 and any neutral or greyish colour would be appropriate.

VENUS rules the fashion world, jewellers, cosmetics, all trades connected with the body. She also rules performers, film and T.V. actors, entertainers, music and the arts. Her jewels and metals are sapphire, alabaster, opals, corals, white pearls and copper. Her animals are the butterfly, the bee, partridges, peacocks, household pets such as goldfish, cats and dogs, etc., singing birds, the sheep and the dove. Venus plants include the birch, the cherry, plum, pear trees, violets, lilac, primula, poppies, strawberries, gooseberries, beans, artichokes, coriander, Easter daisy and periwinkle. The right day for Venus magic is Friday and the night is Monday. Her number is 6 and her proper colour is green.

MARS, of course, governs the armed services, also engineers, dentists and chemists, harpoon and fire-arms manufacturers, metal work, agitators, thieves, rogues and vagabonds, if you call the last three vocations. His jewels and metals are the bloodstone, the garnet, ruby, jasper and iron. His animals include all creatures with stings and poisons, scorpions and venomous snakes, wasps, hornets, etc. Hawks, vultures, beasts of prey such as the hyena, tiger, wolf, also the mule and the donkey. His plants are hops, capers, hemlock, sandalwood, garlic, cactus, thistle, leeks and onions, horseradish, nettles, chives, hawthorn, heather, boxwood, oak, tamarisk, mustard, rhubarb and tobacco. The day for Mars magic is Tuesday and the night is Friday. The number is 9 and the appropriate colour is red.

JUPITER governs government itself and law, the church, teachers, explorers, engineers, discoverers and all sorts of officials. His jewels and metals are the turquoise, lapis-lazuli, dark sapphire, the amethyst and tin. His animals are the crow, the magpie, eagle, lion, deer, dogs, elephants, cows, oxen, buffaloes, horses, weasels, and lizards. His plants include the blueberry, blackberries, eucalyptus, spinach, chicory, cloves, asparagus, anise, rose, cornflower, carnation, the linden tree, the horse chestnut, the chestnut, apricot and fig trees, quince, aloe, colchicum and cedar. The day for Jupiter magic is Thursday and the night is Sunday. The number is 3 and the colour is blue.

SATURN deals with research scientists, farm workers, mine owners, the lead and lumber industry, undertakers and associated professions, stone quarry workers, tannery and leather workers. Saturn's jewels and metals are chalcedony, onyx, black coral, jade, sardonyx, malachite, jet and lead. The appropriate animals include beetles and crustaceans, moles, owls, beavers, pigs, bears, goats, the crane and the ostrich. The correct plants include the holly, mistletoe, ivy, evergreens, pansy, beets, hemp, beech, poplar and palm trees, quince and red oak, weeping willow, mandragora and hemlock, moss, mugwort, aconite. The day for Saturn's magic is, of course, Saturday and the proper night is Tuesday. The number is either 4 or 8 and the colour is black.

Not everyone will agree with the correspondences given here but these were taught to me by the coven of which I was a member. Other covens, other beliefs. Let us now look at some of the recipes of the Craft.

CHAPTER FOUR

Pot Pourri!

It is not my intention to list in full detail any particular formula or remedy involving herbs and plants. Some can be very dangerous. In the event of the reader wishing to experiment with old spells, please be careful. You might have a very unpleasant experience and you could do untold damage. You may or may not achieve your aim. You are sincerely advised to contact an expert in the field, for safety's sake....

The following miscellany is collected at random from books and from witches and there are plenty more recipes where these came from.

To have courage: pluck five teeth from the mouth of a live lion and you shall have no fear (and make sure that the lion doesn't have you!).

Be careful of mishandling parsley for you and yours suffer within the year. (Today in some parts of the country no one will herd parsley for fear of trouble ensuing for the donor or his family.)

Scratch the name of your enemy upon lead using the pin feather of a live bald vulture which has dropped in the hour of Saturn. (Better ask London Zoo for some help on this one.) *Your enemy will die within the next waning moon.*

Ignore the Snowdrop and hurt its feelings and it will not grow the following year.

Along similar lines are very old superstitions about abusing the following wild plants as they are considered to belong to the devil: stitchwort, plantain, sun sponge, shepherds' needles, house leek, yarrow, parsley, wild garlic, aconite, hemlock, and ragwort.

If caught in a storm and you are near an elder tree,

you may shelter beneath its branches safely. (There is an old superstition that the original cross was made from the wood of an elder tree.)

For jaundice, take the roots of ground ivy and boil in water for some time. Let the patient drink some of it to ease his suffering.

If a witch shake her hair loose of all encumbrance when making a curse, it will double the strength of the evil, but take a hair of a sleeping witch and put it in the earth and you nullify the curse.

Rine is a plant that can be thrown at a faithless one to cure unfaithfulness. Clover can be used as an antidote to poison or to aid clearer vision. Rine leaves were used to help in the cure of hydrophobia.

Valerian is used to cure many ills, and shares with mistletoe the name of All Heal. It was and still is used in the cure of nervous disorder, insomnia, cough, etc. It has connections with being used as an aphrodisiac.

The violet has earned its place in the history books for love charms and philters, and as a cure for ulcers. It is sometimes mixed in salads, etc. Infusions of the flower and/or the leaves have been used to cure fevers, jaundice, pleurisy and colds.

Adder's tongue fern is used in lotions and salves for open sores and wounds, and the 'tea' of the leaves is used to aid purification of the blood.

Betony cures haemorrhages, insomnia and fatigue. It is also an aid against visions, bad dreams and drunkenness.

With today's stresses it is not surprising that many people suffer from headaches. You have probably been through the range of proprietary medicines and found them wanting. As an alternative you might do worse than try one of the following:

Camomile tea or laying the head on a pillow stuffed with Camomile flowers.

Wear a violet wreath.

Sage tea or elder tea or boil chrysanthemum roots and drink of the infusion when warm.

Rub horseradish on the forehead, or press mustard leaves against the forehead. (Keep both well away from your eyes.)

Bind the cast-off skin of a snake around the forehead and it will ease the pain.

Traditional witches were supposed to use flying ointment. All the recipes I have been able to trace require ingredients that are both illegal and dangerous. Look them up elsewhere if you must. Don't try them – you've been warned.

Witches also make talismans and charms, since people want charms for all sorts of things. There's no easy step by step guide for making all kinds of talismans, much thought and preparation is necessary. Buying a lucky piece by mail for fifteen pence just will not do for highly personal wants. You have to make the right thing of the right material using the proper tools, you have to make it in the right planetary hour under the right auspices. Here is one example.

A talisman is required to assist a man to hold down his job as a salesman in the Wholesale Canned Goods Industry.

Analysis: The principal ruler here is Mercury with the Moon as a second, though equally important factor. If you cannot afford a silver disc (and Mercury is liquid at normal temperature), then look to the woods ruled by Mercury and then the Moon. Hazel is the obvious choice. It will be fashioned into suitable size, ready for inscription and designs to be engraved upon it at the correct hour.

(Much of this is low magic and not strictly witchcraft but some witches specialize in this sort of thing and it is therefore included.)

You will have to know the Kabbalistic tables for each

planet and their correct signs and sigils. The correct occult alphabet must also be used.

The Divinatory Arts are also not pure Witchcraft, although some of the little used or unknown practices are regarded as such.

We have touched on astrology. Witches occasionally use palmistry, numerology, phrenology, graphology, physiogomy, cartomancy, dice and teacup readings, etc. etc. and etc. You don't have to join a coven to study these subjects but you do need the experience of an adept to guide you through the Craft.

The religious side of the craft is reward enough to the disciples of the faith, but to have the fascination of these richly absorbing subjects in support, makes, what is for them, the most rewarding part of their occult studies.

CHAPTER FIVE

Craft and Priorities

The modern witch is required to know her Book of Shadows – it should be committed to memory. She should be efficient in Astrology, practised in Herbal Lore. She should know seasonal and weather lore, Numerology, Palmistry, Divination, etc. She must be able to make lucky charms, amulets and talismans. She must know her way around Art Magic and Ritual Magic. Above all, she must be able to inspire confidence in those who ask for her help. And she must be able to use psychic powers for healing.

All of which is a tall order for one person. In a modern coven it is usual for one or two members to handle the Astrology, someone else will deal with herbs while another witch instructs on the different facets of the Craft.

The witch is taught that in the old days, the Wise Ones were versed in all the requirements of the Craft and had committed most, if not all of their knowledge to memory.

Because of today's demands, witches have less time for their practices than their predecessors. It is certainly permissible to divide responsibility and achievement. The Astrologer chooses the right time to perform certain ceremonies. He will also select the best moments for constructing talismans and charms. He will decide the right hour for a new member's initiation ceremony so that they exert the correct influences on other coven members. He may also hold classes to instruct others how astrology applies to ritual magic. Possibly he will delay or bring forward a meeting night because of the planetary influences on the day originally selected. He rarely works as a Professional Astrologer for the public. One coven operated without a 'resident' astrologer for some time, availing itself of an Astrologer outside the movement but sympathetic to the cause.

The Herbal or Plant expert with his specialized knowledge is of equal importance and works closely with the Astrologer. All those of my acquaintance have been dedicated followers of Nature for years and their expertise in their beloved work is a wonderful experience to share with them. They give generously of their knowledge, often inheriting their gift from father or mother, rarely referring to the printed word. In this department of the Craft too, decoctions, philters and potions are available in the event of a coven having no practitioner. There are flourishing businesses in their field for anyone who wants to experiment with herbs.

Progress and Spiritual Development are in the hands of the High Priestess and the High Priest. Using exercises, yoga, and their own special methods, they can do much to improve the individual's pyschic capabilities. They will also use invocation and herbal mixtures to induce trances if they feel that their pupil will benefit.

I have known witches to look at you on the first meeting and reel off details about you they could not have known from any other source of information. They will probably tell you something of your 'psychic picture' and, perhaps, a bit about your future. No witch in her right mind will claim to predict all your future with complete accuracy but many people approach them for just such a purpose, thus witches study the different methods of divination.

Apart from Astrology and Palmistry, the principal methods of divination and character assessment, witches study the more obscure methods which have been in use over the years. The Tarot is also used for divination – in my opinion, wrongly. Other methods include Cartomancy – the use of playing cards – and Graphology for character assessment and suitability of career.

Dream interpretation, dice, tea-cups, all these have been used, along with colours and numerology. Precious stones may be cast and the resultant position analysed.

Flowers, and, latterly, the resurgence of interest in the I-Ching has resulted in requests for readings by this method.

Of course the witch is not required to have all this knowledge ready for immediate use. Some of those interested in the spheres of low divination delight in using the more obscure methods, just for appearance's sake. Some of the official interpretations of omens are staggering and some of the methods used are just childish, but all respond to the rule of thumb, 'If it works, use it.'

After all, if you were told by a witch that she used Ceremancy, Metopomancy and Lampadomancy on you, you would have to be impressed and the witch's reputation would grow. You don't know what these mean? :

1 Ceremancy – interpretation of the shape of melting wax dropped on a floor.

2 Metopomancy – interpretation of the lines on your forehead.

3 Lampadomancy – divination from the flame of a lamp.

Witchcraft, however, is fundamentally a religion, and it is the prime concern of all to promote the study of its history, its comparison with other pagan religions and the established church, and its practice.

It was in evidence long before the established Church in this country and some say that it can be traced back to the dawn of time. Witchcraft is a religion of fertility and sympathetic magic plus a constant ambition to develop spiritually, physically and mentally at all times. Into the basic worship of the Moon Goddess and the Horned God has come a form of ritual celebration mixed with Kabbalistic magic and watered-down, pseudo-Egyptian occultism. Certainly Witchcraft today bears no resemblance to the highly imaginative Medieval church publications. All a witch ever needs is the peace that a religion can give. A witch wants to be left alone to enjoy the fruits of the belief and the satisfaction that religious worship can give.

After having studied the history of witchcraft from

both without and within a coven, it is a constant source of amazement to me that it can still flourish. So many anti-witch writings from so many biased and learned people have smeared the movement with malignancy and ignorance that in ordinary circumstances would occasion slander and libel actions. Much of the history of the Craft is concerned with the number of people who died for it. Much more of the history would out-do any book on torture today.

Unfortunately the Craft member selects secrecy. Anything 'secret' cannot be understood in the correct manner, ergo, we have the situation as it has always been. The witch cannot complain too much, for she has selected the path of secrecy.

I am convinced that there is much danger within the 'secrecy' of the Craft. Many practitioners are sincere people who lead normal and blameless lives. They stay within the civil law. They do not work their spells naked on a blasted heath. They do not scourge each other and they do not go in for 'orgies'. Nonetheless they are blamed by press and television for all these things. They are blamed for pushing drugs, seducing the young, corrupting everything, disturbing marriages, causing deaths and so on. They are even blamed for ritual murders.

It is more than time that the 'secrecy' was dropped. It it time that the spells and the Book of Shadows be put under microscopes and examined. Perhaps this book will further a better understanding all round.

PART TWO

The Book of Shadows

I acknowledge the help of the Witch friend Kemoc in dealing with this manuscript.

I owe much to other people within the Craft but their names cannot be mentioned for many reasons.

I also acknowledge the hindrance of a Coven whose Death Curse I have braved in publishing these writings. Their curses didn't help me at all!

Keep the Book of Shadows in your own handwriting. Give to your fellow workers the spells that they need, but your book shall not leave your hands. Hide your book within a secret place and learn from it as much as you can. One day it may become necessary for you to destroy your Book of Shadows, but when the time of necessity is passed, you shall re-write your book with accuracy.

The history of the Craft is a history of persecution and misunderstanding. The possession of a Book of Spells meant torture and death. The burning time is ended long ago but what has happened once may happen once again in time. Yet if a time of persecution shall come once more, see that you do not betray the names of your associates. Remember that in the burning time, others suffered torture rather than betray the Craft and in those days drugs were given them to ease their pain and death came before the fire. And if this history repeats itself, your associates will come to your aid if you betray them not.

Seek not to attract attention for our traditional safety lies in secrecy, and though we made magic, we used common household articles for our craft. Therefore boast not of witch-power. Threaten no man with illness nor evil happenings. Seek not to impress the credulous with strange knowledge but rather hide your secrets from the eyes of those who would not understand. Speak not of the Craft to outsiders and keep the knowledge secret, even in this day.

If you are in trouble, then remember all those who have gone before the God and Goddess and remember their endurance. Confess to nothing if it can be avoided. Remember, if you are questioned by anyone, it is better to speak total foolishness and lies, rather than permit the secret knowledge to be betrayed. It is better to be laughed at rather than suffer another burning time when many people who were not of the Craft were killed by fear and greed.

THE FAITH OF THE CRAFT

We worship the God that men fear, the Horned God of ancient days. We worship the Goddess, the Lady of older times. And the God is the Sun God of life and strength, yet he is also the Dark Lord of peace and understanding. And the Goddess is the Maid of joy and hope. She is the mother of love and protection. Yet she is also the Dark Lady of peace, wisdom and magic. Yet beyond these two, our Lord and our Lady is the One we do not know, that which we cannot name or limit, for the One is limitless.

We work our Craft in the names of the Lord and the Lady. Every spell that we weave, every magic that we work and every act in life is done before these. We carry a part of each within ourselves but the Lord and the Lady are above us. Through our Craft do we serve the Lord and the Lady and do what best we can for our fellow men without the Craft.

ON OBEDIENCE

For as long as you shall remain within the Coven Circle, you shall be obedient to the High Priestess. You shall listen to her words at all times for she is the representative of our Mother, the Goddess and her words are those which rule us.

You shall not fail to obey the command of the High Priestess during any ritual, no matter what the command shall be. The High Priestess is there to aid you and other children of the Goddess, therefore you shall act upon her words, even if you do not immediately see the reason for her instructions.

For between you and the High Priestess there shall be OBEDIENCE.

THE FIVE ESSENTIALS

The most important is INTENTION. You must know what you are there to do and you must know that you will succeed.

You must PREPARE everything properly beforehand and check that it is rightly prepared and that everything lies in readiness.

The Circle must be cast correctly and then purified.

You yourself must be purified, both bodily and spiritually. A ritual bath is a new idea for Craft members but it is a very good idea. And before you start your ceremony you must cast from you hate and malice and any evil that is in you. If this is not done, the ceremony may work very differently to your stated intention.

You must have properly consecrated tools.

THE EIGHTFOLD WAYS

1 Concentration, activated by the firm knowledge that you can and will succeed. Form a clear picture in your mind of all your requirements accomplished

2 Trance states – these include the use of clairvoyance and astral travel

3 Herbal knowledge, incense and wine

4 Performing rites with a purpose

5 The use of the dance

6 The use of chants and spells

7 Body control

8 Total involvement in worship

THE GREATER AND LESSER SABBATS

The sabbats are MAY EVE – 30th April – sometimes called Roodmass, Roodday and Walpurgis night though the last name is, strictly speaking a German name and never used in this country. There is a Sabbat on November Eve which is known to the Craft as Souwain and to the Christians as Hallowe'en. Between these come Candlemas (2nd February) and the Gales of August, also known as Lammas.

The Solstices and Equinoxes are also celebrated by Craft members, the first day of spring, midsummer day, the beginning of autumn and the shortest day of the year. Actually the dates of these days vary and are best looked up in a diary.

The Esbat was the Small Assembly which took place at the local meeting point, primarily for business purposes, cures, local magic and 'any other business', whereas the Sabbat was usually religious, the one exception to this rule being May Eve, this being the time of feasting and merriment.

The primitive manner of life was a constant battle for survival against an environment which was seldom over-generous. Food was the first necessity of life and, as man learned to hunt, the woman became protector, healer, mother and nurse. In a fortified village settlement it was the woman's responsibility to acquire and pass on the knowledge of healing herbs, etc. Hence she became the prototype of the Mother Goddess who symbolizes Rest, Pleasure, Contentment, Love and Life.

FESTIVALS

In some of the festivals in the olden days, when the meeting was held a little distance away from the village, it was a custom to bring at least one broomstick to the meeting. The purpose behind the custom was the use of the broomstick as something to jump over – the higher you jumped, the higher the corn would grow and so the better the harvest. However, in the general 'horseplay' and merry-making, the broomstick was ridden or used as a dancing partner. This gave rise to the legend that all witches rode broomsticks.

It was also customary to have seasonal branches and flowers at a Craft meeting, i.e. blossoms in Maytime, green branches in August, autumn leaves at Hallowe'en or evergreens at Candlemas.

One must remember that the traditions of the Craft date back to the time before street lighting and cars. A

Craft meeting place that was half a mile away from the village was considered far away from anywhere. It was safe to light a fire in such a place, and one could make a noise without being noticed. No policemen would appear to see what was going on and, in a civilization based on sunrise-sunset, it was perfectly safe to meet at midnight, so long as you were home at sunrise. It was a matter of safety.

Sweet smelling herbs and woods were always thrown into the fire before and after the dancing. Today it is seldom possible to dance in the open air and very often the space available in modern houses and flats makes dancing impossible anyway.

MISCELLANEOUS NOTES

It is a common belief that witches cast love spells and there are all sorts of recipes purporting to cause love between two people. In strict Craft law it is not considered legal to force an unwilling woman or man into love by use of a spell, though this ruling might be waived to force a hesitant lover to make a proposal of marriage, etc. It's not considered legal to deprive another person of his or her will and there are many witches who would argue against mending a marriage if it appeared that both parties would be happier elsewhere. Craft members were supposed to know the plants with aphrodisiac powers. They were also supposed to know the plants which could cause abortions and, whilst there are different ethics on this last problem, it was reckoned a useful accomplishment in war torn lands where rape was a common occurrence.

The Esbat is the Small Assembly of the local coven. It is sometimes held at the full of the moon and sometimes at the new moon.

A man is usually initiated into the Craft by a woman and a woman is usually initiated by a man. Exceptions to this rule crop up from time to time where a solitary man or woman, perhaps not in contact with any other member of the Craft, instructs one of the same sex in useful spells.

Occasionally at a Craft meeting a man is asked to represent the God and a woman is asked to represent the Goddess. The key word is 'represent' – it does not mean imitate!

The original concern of the Craft was the fertility of the land – the ever present problem of food and its storage. Today this has taken 'second place' for many Craft members are city dwellers who leave scientists and agricultural experts to deal with these problems. However, the problems were associated with a High Priestess of the Craft. She had to be a skilled lady, able to say what the weather would do. She had to know everything about which seeds to sow and when to harvest them and she was probably the oldest woman present at the gathering. This custom has given rise to the idea that witches were old women on broomsticks but the oldest woman was always supposed to be wise in her ways.

Ever remember that it is the duty of those in the Craft to help those who ask for aid, if help can be given.

The traditional colour of the witches is green, considered by many outside the Craft to be an unlucky colour.

Remember that when we are within the circle of the Craft, what happens within the circle is the concern of both worlds.

Keep your clothing for the Craft in a secret place and wear it not for any lesser worship. Let it be clean and well prepared for sudden usage. And before you put on your clothing, remember that you put from you your ordinary self. And you put on the robe of the Craft, asking the Lord and the Lady that you be clean of heart for you do their work.

Although it is in no way essential, some Craft women wear a ceremonial bracelet. This is always made of silver and usually about 2″ broad. It is often engraved with a Craft name in one of the secret scripts, together with the proper signs of rank or the sign of the pentagram.

SCOURGING

Though this is not a part of our native Craft, there are those of the Craft who feel that it must be done, the men receiving it first and the women afterwards. There are various ideas about the number of strokes to be given though it usually means forty. Scourging is in direct conflict with the CHARGE which states that one does not harm one's own body or any other body, these being the gift of the Lord and the Lady.

TO GET THE SIGHT

Every child is born with the magical sight yet some children reject that sight for themselves and some are punished for seeing the spiritual world. Discouraging a child from having magical sight is regarded as a crime, but occasionally a Craft member will counsel a child not to speak of all it sees, lest the child bring trouble on its own head.

The adult who desires to increase sight often does it with the help of meditation and incense. Each one endeavours to relax and allow the atmosphere to build up, using music and incense to stimulate the senses. There are many incenses that can be bought today and many more recipes that appear in obscure books of learning. Yet the witch must ever remember that vision is not reality and the two must never be confused.

THE MEETING DANCE

The dance is led by a man or a maiden, depending on the ceremony, but whichever shall lead, the other shall follow alternately, man and woman. It is reckoned that a dance that follows the path of the sun is the proper way and the dance that runs against the sun is a dance of evil.

THE COMMEMORATIVE DANCE

If a dance is done to commemorate an event in the past, it must be done not simply as a representation of the event but to make all those present remember everything that was involved. You must dance your magical purpose, and you must dance it with feeling and desire. Mime dances are an ancient tradition, lost in the dawn of time. Those that have come down to us in English folk-lore are sometimes confused and require careful research. It is better not to mime some forgotten battle and misinterpret a dance, for the misinterpretation will bring about unhappy results. Rather mime some new dance than follow an ancient formula that means something very different to your desire.

THE TOOLS OF THE CRAFT

From the dawn of time, Craft members have made their own tools and it is right to do so. It is not always possible to make your own equipment, but even if you buy your tools, you alone must consecrate them.*

THE ALTAR

Traditionally this is a small table such as is found in any household. If it is possible, let your altar be kept apart and not used for any other thing. Yet if this is not possible, then cover the table with a clean white cloth and put only a vase of flowers upon it. Use not this table for anything save for your craft workings.

THE SECRET PLACE

Of old those who followed the Craft were taught to hide the tools of their work within some secret place. If possible this should be near to where you sleep but be certain that the tools of the Craft are locked away and let no one touch them. Your tools are not loaned to others within the Craft, they are not given, save for the cup and this must be given with love. You shall not use tools that are bought in the market place but are not new, for you know not who has used those tools. Nor shall you in-

* One exception to this rule. You never buy your cup – it's always a present from another Craft member.

herit tools from any unknown source. But, having your own tools, you shall keep them in a secret place and ask protection that your secret is not discovered lest it bring trouble upon you.

INCENSE

For good results it is best to buy a proper incense. Traditionally we make our own incense from sweet smelling herbs such as rosemary, thyme and basil. A chafing dish of hot coal is used for burning the herbs. Use not a censer for, though these can be bought, they are not a part of the Craft and may lead to the accusation that you have robbed a church.

THE CUP AND THE PLATTER

During the time of the persecutions, no special magical equipment was marked or set aside in any way, lest a search reveal it. The cup used in a Craft ceremony was simply the best cup in the household and the platter likewise. They were not made of silver or gold lest we were accused of withholding taxes or thieving from the Church. Nor were the Cup and Platter marked in any way outwardly, but rather consecrated with the sign of the Pentagram drawn upon them in charged water and that way they were sacred to the Lord and the Lady from that time forth. Today the Cup and the Platter are made of the best materials you can afford and hidden away in a secret place to be used only in the Cakes and Wine ceremony.

THE ATHAME

'Athame' is the word for a black handled knife used in Craft working. Of old it was the most useful tool in a household. It was made of iron with a handle which should be of box wood. It was not marked with any sign but today's knives are often marked in secret writings and with signs of power.

THE WHITE HANDLED KNIFE

This is essential to some Craft members. It is likewise made of iron and put away until it is needed.

THE SWORD

Traditionally you had no sword unless you had actually fought in a war, for the presence of a sword in a household where Witchcraft was suspected would have damned the household. Nor are names of power engraved upon the sword for this would have been held as evidence of trafficking with the devil. In fact the sword is simply an extension of the knife and not strictly necessary to the practising Craft member. Remember that a sword engraved with magical signs cannot easily be concealed and a consecrated sword must not be drawn without greatest care.

THE WAND

This you shall cut yourself using the consecrated athame. You shall go out before dawn on Midsummer day and choose a proper tree to cut it from as the sun arises. Or you shall cut your wand when the stars are most propitious to you. And having cut the wand, you shall take it in a bag and let none see or handle it, before or after it is consecrated.

THE SCOURGE

This is not a part of our tradition. If you desire to make such a thing, you shall cut a stick and bind it with cords. Let there be eight cords and each cord shall be knotted five times.

THE PENTACLE

The Pentacle is the sign of the Craft, the five-pointed star sign. Sometimes this is engraved on a flat plate of copper which is used for the Cakes and Wine ceremony. It used to be drawn on a plate in ink and washed off immediately after use as the possession of such an object would be deemed proof of bad magic. Today it can be engraved on a sheet of copper or even a silver plate.

TO MARK OUT A CIRCLE

In order to mark out a new circle, measure out a cord that it shall be 4′ 6″ with a loop at one end. Place your athame, point downwards, in the centre of the ground or room and slip the loop over the handle of the knife. Using the length of cord as a radius, draw out the circle in the ground and then retrace the circle using the athame. Always renew the circle as you use it but you can have it permanently marked out on private ground so that it is always in the same place.

Remember that the circle, being properly made and consecrated, must prevent the magical power from being dissipated instead of being applied. The circle holds the power in.

The circle is also a protection against disturbing and mischievous forces. Whilst it is being prepared, a 'gateway' is left in the circle for members to enter. Once the circle is completed, no one may enter or leave until the ceremony is ended.

Always remember that Craft workings are best done collectively by a number of associates who feel the same emotions.

The earliest Craft rituals were more concerned with food than anything else for food meant survival. Our ancestors sought the aid of the Lord and the Lady within the circle with that end in mind. They desired most sincerely to multiply plants, animals and children. Ritual bridges the gulf between real life and total worship. The original aims have passed for today's Craft members, yet the Craft has broadened and become a study and the rituals must be regarded in the light of the changing days.

It is essential to maintain order and discipline at a meeting, if worship is to be done or if anything is to be accomplished. Harken and heed the words of the Priestess or Priest who presides over the meeting, lest it degenerate into disorder.

The Lord and the Lady alone see the true colours of each heart and know who merits punishment and who shall have praise. Only They have the right to punish the faults of a coven member. Yet if a member of the Craft has caused trouble within the circle, it is better to bid that person be gone rather than cause evil to him. Justice and Mercy are not in your hands. You are not the God or the Goddess, therefore seek not to punish but leave such things unto those whom we worship.

Remember that we do not seek to be the enemy of any man. We strive to be the friend of that which IS eternally.

We seek no quarrel with any man but rather we seek that quarrels may be swiftly reconciled.

We seek not to devise evil against any being, man, woman or animal. If anyone shall devise evil against us, we seek to escape without harm and without the need of hurting those who plot against us.

May we seek to attain only those things which are good and true and considered to be the blessings of the Ancient Ones, LOVE, FREEDOM, HAPPINESS AND PEACE.

ON SAFE WORKING IN THE CIRCLE

For your own safety, consider well the following rules that are written by one with great experience.

1 If you will work in the open, then ascertain that none can oversee you for surely gossip will spread a lying report of that which you do and this will cause trouble to practitioners of the Craft.

2 If you work within a house, then make sure that it is empty of other humans and, when you have finished your ritual, close down the power lest others take fright at the nearness of the unseen world.

3 Design your robes for the Craft as simply as possible, remembering that you may be dancing in those robes – they must not be overlong to trip you up. Sleeves should be fairly tight so that nothing is knocked off the altar.

Cloaks are made to conceal the identity of the wearer but masks, if worn, may impede the vision. Tall hats, à la fairy-tale type of witch, will come off in a wind unless tied firmly on the head! They also come off when dancing!

4 Before commencing any ceremony, make certain that everything you need is within the witch's circle. Apart from the basic initiation where someone is sent to fetch a candidate, no one ever leaves a circle in the middle of a ritual. It is bad technique and it can be very dangerous.

5 Fire is not the only element that can cause trouble, all of them can get out of control. But fire is a spectacular trouble maker if there is an angry elemental behind it. Candles must be firmly in place before you start your ceremony. Bonfires out of doors must be properly controlled. It is a good idea to wear fireproof clothing. It is also a good idea to have a proper fire extinguisher within the circle. Take no chances with fire.

6 Bowls of coal and incense – they do get hot over a period of time, especially if the bowl is made of metal. Metal bowls can burn human skin and also char the altar. You might try up-dating tradition here by consecrating an asbestos plate and putting the fire-bowl on that and not touching it, once the incense is alight. Some covens use a censer – this isn't traditionally a Craft instrument but occasionally you come across the rite which requires one to walk around the circle a number of times, censing it as one goes. Obviously carrying a burning hot plate of coals and incense is not practical so a censer is used for this sort of proceeding. Censers, however, are tricky to work. They get tangled up and they can spill burning charcoal. The best rule is to insist that everyone stands still while the censer is used. Only one person moves and he or she goes three times round the circle or nine times or however many times you feel necessary. When you finish with the censer, hang it up out of the way. Like the plate it gets too hot to leave it standing on an altar and

the chains get tangled. Do it properly or don't use a censer at all!

7 Cleaning tools and temple silver or copper is a job that gets done by a member of the coven, not by an outsider. Do not clean a metal cup with a cyanide-based polish if you or anybody else intend to drink from that cup. Wash it and polish with elbow grease instead! Varnish is a new invention and very useful on silver plate – use it.

8 Make arrangements that, in case of accident, another coven member has access to your tools. All sorts of troubles crop up when the instruments of the Craft turn up on a stall in Portobello Road as second-hand curios. The general public handle those curios without knowing what they are. If you cannot dispose of your own tools and robes, someone else of your tradition must be able to do so for you.

9 'Please' and 'Thank you' are words of power. You cannot command the Lord to do what you want. You cannot threaten the Goddess with anything. If you try to bully, command, browbeat, threaten or bribe the unseen world, you will convince the unseen world that you're stupid! Ask for something, by all means, and remember that 'No' is an answer, even if it isn't the one that you want. Thank the Powers that have aided you when you've finished.

10 If you're dealing with an unfamiliar ceremony, take the time to rehearse beforehand. Don't 'rush' through it because someone wants to take an early train home. A coven member in bad health does not dance or exert himself because you do NOT want a corpse on your hands, nor do you want anyone passing out during the ceremony. Allow a certain amount of time at the end of the ceremony for power to 'die down'. It is NOT good technique to leave a place magically 'alive' – it frightens the skin off ordinary human beings. Close your ceremony properly when the working is finished and may the Lord and Lady bless you.

SUCCESS

You shall remember that the success or failure of any operation lies not in the tools that you have but rather in the mental attitude of the operator. If you are not keyed up to high pitch when you work your ceremony, you will not attain success.

THE PURPOSE

You shall state the purpose of your ceremony clearly that all present may know the object in view and desire the object most dearly. The simple tools described will aid you and, properly consecrated, they are an extension of yourself. They are not regarded as outside objects or 'curiosities', they are a part of you and all your power and they should be near you always. The Athame should lie beneath your pillow for months. (Today's witch carries an athame in her handbag or briefcase.) No one handles your tools save you yourself, the exception to this rule being a pair of Craft members living and working together. They may use the same tools.

THE PATTERN

The majority of Craft workings conform to a pattern. When all are met and the circle is prepared, the High Priestess stands before the altar, raises her hands in a gesture of invocation and says 'Let the ceremony begin.'

There is always a prayer for protection.

There is a 'statement of purpose'.

Any special magical working follows and then comes the seasonal celebration.

Initiations are usually followed by cakes and wine.

There is often a pause for 'any other business' – healing a sick animal, a prayer for a sick child to get over chickenpox quickly, it is usually something that a Craft member would like help with but not something big enough to be the main purpose of the ritual.

Announcements are made – maybe even the date, time and place of the next meetings are read out.

Finally a closing prayer is read by the High Priestess who then says, 'Before the God and the Goddess, the meeting is ended.'

Though the formal Craft meeting is ended, many of the workings are followed by a feast or party of some kind, and possibly even dancing.

INVOCATION AND CONSECRATION OF THE CIRCLE

First draw the Circle with the Athame or sword. Consecrate salt and water as follows:

Be this salt dedicated to the Lord and the Lady to keep us from evil and to protect us in this time.

Be this water dedicated to the Lord and the Lady to keep us from peril and to purify this place.

Mix the salt and water together and sprinkle sunwise around the circle.

May we cast from us all evil and darkness, viciousness and malice. May we become that which we must be before the Lord and the Lady, seeking ill to no one. May we be clean within and without so that we are acceptable before Them.

Invocations should start in the East and proceed SUNWISE, ending at the North for this reason: the North is the place of power which flows from North to South. The operator, being in the East, works up to the right. Having reached the North point, the Circle must still be closed so that there is no gap in it. The DEOSIL movement works up to the height. A WIDDERSHINS movement works downwards and is a movement of bad magic, cursing and so on.

The INVOCATION to form the circle is thus:

Oh Mighty Powers of the East, I call upon you in this place and at this hour to keep safe our Circle and guard and look upon these works.

Draw the invoking pentagram in the air:

Now move to the South and repeat the invocation, only of course you invoke the Powers of the South. Draw the pentagram. Repeat this procedure to the West and the

North and then turn and face the East once more before you go to the ALTAR.

Candles should be in place at the North, South, East and West and you have learned to consecrate the fire upon the altar. From this are lit the candles of the quarters at this stage.

An invocation is made to protect the Circle as follows:

Now the sacred Lady rises
New within the starlit sky,
Now before the esbat meeting
Guard us, lady, by and by.
Wrap us in the cloak of darkness,
Hide us in the mist of time.
Ere the spell is brewed and settled
Hide us till the morning chime.
Guide us ere the dance commences,
Hide the cakes, conceal the wine,
Lead us in the age of darkness,
Sacred queen and all Divine.

Guard us, Lord of Hunt and forest,
By the powers of fire and air,
As we come once more to worship,
Keep us, Witch Lord, in your care.
By the power of earth and water
Now the circle spins and spins,
Come unto the secret servants,
Guard us, now the Rite begins.

After this invocation for protection, it is proper that the chafing dish of coals and incense shall be carried around the circle. Such covens as insist on the use of the scourge will now use it. All now dance around the altar using an invoking chant:

Thrice about the altar go
Once for virgin, pure as snow,
Once for full moon's soft sweet breath,

Once for dark moon, old as death,
Thrice about the altar spin
That the rite shall well begin.

Then shall be said the petition that everyone shall know the purpose of the ritual.

Witch Lord, Witch Lady, Sacred Pair that were before the dawn of time and shall be till the dusk, hear now the purpose of this ritual and witness it. For the ceremony is performed that ... (Briefly and clearly state the purpose of the ritual.)

Now to end the meeting, you shall do the same circling movement starting in the East and saying to the four quarters, *Mighty Powers of the East, I thank you for guarding this circle and for keeping us safe at this time and we bless thee in the Name of the Lord and the Lady, in the Name* ZARACH *and in the name* ZARUNA. You proceed to each quarter with your Athame or sword but you do NOT draw the pentagram.

Sometimes the request to the powers of the quarters is made as follows:

Before the Lord and the Lady I call upon the Spirits of the East that they come unto us to witness our sacred rites in the Name of Zarach and in the Name of Zaruna.

When the circle is formed, the directions North, South, East and West, should be marked with candles. These are called the candles of the quarters.

In some covens where the scourge is used, the High Priestess enters the circle from the South West with her scourge in her left hand and her Athame in her right hand. She moves clockwise around the circle to the East and stops, holding the instruments outstretched in the pentacle position. The rest of the coven enter for their ritual scourging and then the High Priestess draws the circle and carries on as before.

THE CLOSING OF THE CIRCLE

High Priestess (except possibly at Lammas when this

may well be said by the High Priest): 'Companions, we have met together this night to celebrate the ... Feast. Together we have worked for our purposes. The God and the Goddess have witnessed our workings and only they will measure all our purposes and all our hearts. Together we have invoked for power to accomplish our working but it is not for us to command those whom we worship. Nor is it for us to bid them to be gone. We cannot dismiss them. I ask instead of Zarach and Zaruna that they are with us all our days, guiding our feet and lighting our paths. I ask that the Lord and the Lady are with us in our lives and in our deaths, our true parents, even as we are their children. Let the circle be extinguished but let us not forget our working of this night. Let the candles be put out but let us not forget what we have learned. Let the rite be ended now in the knowledge that we shall meet once more.

'Before the Lord and the Lady, Zaruch and Zaruna, God and Goddess, the meeting is ended.'

PETITION POEM

Lord of hunt and Shining Queen
Hear the word the witches speak,
Speak the words the witches know,
Now within the midnight hour,
Grant us, Lord and Lady, power!

See upon the altar now,
Cord and incense, wand and knife,
Cup and flame and water clear,
Cakes and wine for feasting hour,
Grant us, Lord and Lady, power.

Horned hunter, Lady Moon,
See the spell becomes complete,
Take the wish behind the rite
Bless it in this meeting hour,
Grant it, Lord and Lady, POWER!

CALLS

There were many chants and songs used in the gatherings and dances of ancient days. The meanings of many of these chants are forgotten but we know they used cries of:

ARE – OW ARE – OW ARE – OW

and

IR – AY, IR – AY, IRU – TAI

Also was used

ALAB – AUOOO

and

PIRTU!

Other calls are

OMORF – OR – EN

and

CROYKA

CHANTS

'FAI, FAI, KUN OT KAL
FIR, FIR, KUN IT KAL
KLEET, FIR, KUN OT KAL
CROYA, CROYA, CROYKA'

'SEMA, SEMA, SEMA,
META HARU TEI
IBOX 'ARMAGH TE
QUA OI ZIRE'

These are two ancient chants whose meaning are perhaps lost forever. A more modern Craft love chant is as follows:

I sew your shadow with my hair,
I bind your shadow unto me,
By day or night you shall remain
Before the Triple Goddess three,
I bind your shadow unto me.
Maiden, Mother, Hecate,
Dawn and noon and night black sea,

Free thou art but bound to me,
And thou art mine eternally.

A consecration of fire runs as follows:

Be to me the fire of moon,
Be to me the fire of night,
Be to me the fire of joy,
Turning darkness into light,
By the virgin waxing cold,
By the mother, full and bold,
By the hag queen, silent, old,
By the moon, the one in three,
Consecrated, BLESSED BE.

Craft tradition includes scarf magic – putting a spell on a scarf to keep the wearer safe, or even to strangle the wearer! This spell is used to send a scarf in search of a missing person.

Cloth twine and scarf creep,
Cloth search and cloth seek,
Scarf spelled and Scarf blest,
Aid and guide me in my quest.
Scarf move and scarf search,
Scarf look and cloth lurch.
Scarf turn and twist and run,
Hoop and twine the spell begun,
Scarf of past and present bind,
Seek and search and search to find.

One of the Craft powers is that of working with illusions. Witches were supposed to cause storms at sea but few people know that Craft members can make a phantom fleet of ships like that which appeared on D-Day. This is a Chant which could well have been used for that operation:

Wind and water, moon and sea,
Make the phantom ships for me.
Moon and water, loose the sail,
Pass the fleet with sea swept gale,

Heave the ships in salt drenched spray,
Moonlit mass have ships today.
Wind and moonlight, wind and dark,
Build a fleet of phantom barque,
Moon and water, wind and wave,
Carry phantom ships to save.
Wind and moonlight, storm and gale,
Creak the timbers, furl the sail,
Ghostly inmates serve the swell,
Man the ships that serve me well.
Moon and water, dark and free,
Guide my ships across the sea
Sail the ships tonight for me.

Another love chant used by witches:

Dance the circle dance of dreaming,
Lonely by the crystal sea,
Spin the web of mist and moonlight,
Come, beloved, and follow me.

Chant the chant of souls entwining
Round and through the sacred fire,
Drink from wells of mist and moonshine,
Lover, come to Love's desire.

Dream the dreams of solemn passion
Through the star encrusted night,
Weave the web of mist and moonfire,
Loved one, know all love's delight.

Hear the tides, the heaving waters,
Sombre on the crystal sand,
Hear the chant of longing, waiting,
Come, fulfil at love's demand.

Seek and love my waiting body,
Waiting nightly by the sea,
Tread the path of mist and moonlight,
Lover, come, beloved, to me.

USE OF THE SWORD

Let it ever be remembered that a properly consecrated sword of the Craft must not lightly be unsheathed, lest it bring quarrels and misfortune among those present. Use not the sword to impress others for it is better to have no sword than to bring trouble amongst your associates or to unsheath it in an unjust quarrel.

ANCIENT SYMBOLISM

The Pentagram – this is the symbol of the Craft and the star of our hope; though others also seek the star, this sign is our own.

The Cross in various patterns and variations is a very ancient symbol but it symbolizes Deity and man and the relationship between the two.

The triangle, the geometrical sign of the three in one is another ancient symbol. The triangle with apex pointed upwards symbolized the male and used with the point downwards it is the female sign.

The Poles, Pillars, etc., are the ancient symbols of the creative forces of nature. Shafts, pylons, monolithic stones and so on are of phallic origin.

The Circle is a symbol of eternity, that without beginning or ending. It is sometimes known as the Ring.

The Celtic Cross – or circle divided into four equal quarters – is the division of the elements, the basic compass, the cycle of birth and death and so on.

FRUIT, PLANT AND TREE SYMBOLS

The oak is the tree of our power, as the willow tree is the one from which we weave bewitchment. The holly is the tree of the blood as the hazel tree is the bearer of the fruit of wisdom. The apple tree is the tree for lovers but the evergreen trees, the elder and the yew were the trees of death.

But if you would bring an offering to the goddess at Beltane, then bring to Her blossoms and spring flowers. And if there is an offering at Lammas, then let it be of green branches and summer flowers. If there is an offering at Samhain, let it be ripe fruit and autumn leaves. And if you offer plant life at Candlemas, then the plants are evergreen and winter flowers.

WORDS OF THE MIGHTY ONE

Keep your silence amidst the noise of the world for there is my peace in that silence.

Keep peace between yourself and other beings and listen to all men. Even the ignorant among mankind may perceive a truth you do not see. Surrender not your spirit to any other, yet seek not battle but rather seek to avoid those people who trouble your spirit and spread vexation about them.

Seek not ambition too closely, for the most humble work must also be done and properly done, this pleases the Lord and Lady.

Those of the Craft are as your brothers.

Speak not of the Craft to the outsider for the world is plagued with misunderstanding. But remember that the world also has its virtues and ideals, and its people have their right also to seek for Deity.

Strive to be gentle and understanding with your fellow men and be tolerant of their emotions, even if you do not understand them.

Regard the passing of the years without despair. Surrender the things of youth without sorrow, for age shall bring you deeper wisdom and greater understanding.

Study, then, the secret ways and cultivate the spiritual strength to shield you in unexpected misfortune.

Seek not to harm your own body, nor the body of any man or woman or child or animal, for all bodies are made of the substance of the earth and you shall not harm the earth mother. Therefore be gentle with yourself, for you are a child of the God and the Goddess.

Therefore care for your body, keeping it clean and healthy.

Disgrace not the Craft before your fellow men and bring not disrepute upon its followers.

Remember that you have walked this world before and shall walk it again in time. You may fill this world with broken dreams and sadness and these shall stay with you for many lives. Yet this world is beautiful, though you are blind to its beauty.

Therefore be careful. Seek and be happy. Blessed be.

CONSECRATION OF A SWORD OR ATHAME

If possible partake of the cakes and wine.

High Priest and High Priestess say together: *I conjure thee, O sword that thou shalt serve me as a strength and a defence in every magical ceremony. You shall defend me against my enemies both visible and invisible. In the Name of Zarach and Zaruna.* (The High Priestess immerses the sword or Athame in charged water after which the High Priest passes the instrument through smoking incense. They both speak again:)

I conjure thee again in the Holy Name of Zarach and Zaruna, O Sword, serve me in adversity for my protection. So aid me now. (The sword is laid with another consecrated sword upon the altar. The unconsecrated sword should be consecrated by an experienced craft member who picks up the already consecrated weapon and presses with it on the other. The High Priestess and High Priest say together:)

I conjure thee, O creature of steel, by the God and the Goddess whom we worship, by the waters and the winds, by the earth and by the fire, that in your virtue I shall attain my desire. Come when I call thee by this new name ... (name the instrument) *by the power of Zarach and Zaruna.*

If a sword and Athame have to be consecrated at the same time, then the High Priest will press the sword to the sword and the High Priestess will press the Athame to the new Athame. Both Sword and Athame are then pressed to each other and then placed on the altar. When this ceremony is finished the weapon, or weapons, are picked up by their new owner and must be pressed against the body for some time. Ultimately the Athame becomes an extension of the witch so it must remain constantly with the owner for at least one month. No one else may touch your working tools as they are, strictly speaking, your own body and a part of yourself. You control your own tools all the time lest others work evil through you. A pair of Craft members, working together, can use the same tools, which become a mixture of both.

CONSECRATION OF OTHER TOOLS (i.e. the white handled knife, the wand, the pentacle and the scourge if you use it. All these must be consecrated and blessed separately.)
Zarach and Zaruna, deign to bless this white handled knife which I would consecrate and set aside. Let it obtain the necessary virtues for acts of beauty and love in the names of the Lord and the Lady.
(The white handled knife or other instrument is then immersed in charged water, dried and held in the smoke of incense.)
Zarach and Zaruna, I call upon thee to bless this instrument which I have prepared in thine honour.
(Repeat the water and incense smoke. Hold the instrument high in the air and say:)
Let blessing be.
(Try to use the new tool as soon as possible.)

PREPARING THE CAKES AND WINE

The Cakes

These must be made of meal, salt, wine and honey. They should be shaped like a crescent moon. Put them to bake saying:

Let the cakes be baked in the name of Zaruna for now is the time of the ... feast when the secret worshippers meet once more. Before the Goddess we shall drain the cup. Before the Goddess we shall serve the secret rites.

Before the Goddess we shall feast and rejoice. In the Holy Name of Zaruna and in the Holy Name of Zarach.

The Wine

This should be home-made white wine, placed on the altar in a glass jug.

Let the wine be made ready in the name of Zarach and in the name of Zaruna. Let it be placed upon the altar beneath the sign of the pentagram that the worshippers shall drink of it. Before our God and Goddess, we shall consume and be consumed by the wine of wisdom and blessing. Before the Lord and the Lady we shall consume the cakes and the wine. Before Zarach and Zaruna.

THE CAKES AND THE WINE CEREMONY

The cakes and wine are placed upon the altar.

The High Priestess goes to the altar and then turns to face the High Priest who has followed her. He may kiss her feet, knees and stretch out his arms in a gesture of adoration or he may simply hold out his hands in a gesture of petition and say:

Before our secret queen, Zaruna, Lady of Night, give blessing on this food that it will bring us the fulfilment of all that we desire.

The High Priestess replies, *The secret blessing is given.*

The High Priest takes the cup of wine and offers it to the High Priestess. She takes up her Athame and places the point in the cup, saying:

Health, joy, strength, peace, love, these are the gifts of those whom we follow, Zarach and Zaruna.

The High Priestess lays the Athame on the altar. She takes the cup in both hands and drinks. Then she offers it to the High Priest. The High Priest takes the plate of cakes and holds them out. The High Priestess blesses each cake with the moistened blade of the Athame. She then cuts one cake in half and shares it with the High Priest. He distributes the cakes to the other coven members and returns the plate. He bows or kisses and adores.

THE INVOCATION OF THE GOD

The High Priest stands before the altar facing the South. In one hand he holds the sword and in the other hand he holds the wand.

The High Priestess faces him carrying her wand with which she invokes, saying:

Giver of Life and strength, Giver of Plenty, Witch-Lord, Zarach, thou who art also the Lord of the Path of Death and peace, Descend, I call thee, unto the body of thy servant and priest . . .

Using the wand, the High Priestess draws the Pentacle sunwise upon the body of the High Priest. This is followed by the five-fold salute.

All the coven members bow.

THE INVOCATION OF THE GODDESS

The High Priestess stands before the altar, facing South. In one hand she carries the Athame and in the other she carries the cup (or sometimes the scourge). The High Priest faces her bearing the Wand with which he invokes, saying:

I invoke and call upon thee, Three-fold Goddess of the moon, Zaruna of the secret name. Queen of the moonlit sea, fairer than night and silver-clad, thee I invoke. Mother of the moon and calm waters, let thy light fall upon us for thy hair is a pool of stars in the darkness, I call upon thee. Widow of the waning moon whose children have grown and left thee to sorrow, guard us with learning and grant us a place in thy dark cloak of understanding. Thee I invoke. Descend, I call thee, unto the body of thy servant and priestess . . .

The High Priest draws the sign of the pentacle sunwise upon the body of the Priestess. This is followed by the five-fold salute.

This ceremony is frequently known as 'Drawing Down the Moon'. References to it by this name appear in many newspaper clippings and occult fiction books.

THE CHARGE

'Hear now the words of the Great Mother who has been called un-numbered names. Hear now the counsel of Zaruna, for she has said, I have been with you from the beginning of time and I shall be with you beyond its ending, for I am time. You shall come to me in silence for I know all of your needs and desires.

You shall gather before me, openly or secretly, by day or by night. I am your Queen and I only, yet to my faithful servants have I taught much wisdom, if you will endure.

To those who follow not the secret ways, you shall conceal from them the secrets of your wisdom. But strive to deal with them fairly for many there are who worship me in some other name, and many know me not.

Keep unsullied your ideals and yet respect the ideals of other beings, for many people strive for other greatnesses and their lives also are touched with glory.

Grant to your friends within the Craft and without the Craft, your love and best words and cheer. Betray them not but give to them only happiness at your hands.

Seek not quarrels and warfare, not for any reason. Such reasons as there are for warfare are born of phantasies and fears. Rather seek out reasons for a mutual respect and enjoy together the manifold possibilities of life.

Seek out spiritual strength and council that you will not be overwhelmed by sudden misfortune.

Be gentle with your body and not severe, for I have given you your body as a gift and you are my own child. Nor seek to maim the body of your foe for I have created him, also.

Keep peace with yourself and hold honour dearly in your own heart, for this is the way of peace unto me.

Feign not affection, nor love where there is no love. Part willing from those who are a vexation unto you.

Fear not the passing of the years, for there is wisdom not in my youthful countenance, but in my darker face. Fear not life, for you shall remember that the wheel of death and rebirth shall level all things in the end.

Fear not death, for as you are my own true servant, I shall enfold you in my cloak and you shall sleep until another dawn.

My servant, remember that though this world shall seem a place of sadness and evil, corruption and devastation, yet I have made this world most beautiful and you, also.

Therefore accept that which life shall bring you. Live it and know all of my beauty.

For know that I am she who spun this world. I am the changeless and ever changing goddess, Zaruna, Queen of Heaven. I am she who is crowned with the stars. My cloak covers all men and my voice is the whisper of the midnight winds.

O my beloved servant, come to me secretly. Worship me in silence and I will give you multitudes of blessings. Whatever life shall bring to you, I promise you ecstasy in an ending of all desire. Call, therefore on the name of Zaruna, your Queen, and you shall come to me.'

THE CEREMONY FOR CANDLEMAS

Strictly speaking this is a ceremony for women and men may or may not be invited in. The women set out the circle and prepare it with early spring flowers if possible. They light the lamps or candles and invoke for the Goddess to come to them. They welcome her and install her, possibly on a special 'throne' which has been decorated for the festival. They deal with any business which cannot be done when men are present. After this the High Priestess asks whether the men shall be permitted to enter. If the women decide in favour of the men, the men are called in to adore the Goddess and hear some secret of women's magic. Cakes and wine may be distributed and feasting and dancing may end the festival.

Candlemas invocation (done by the High Priestess):

Queen and Lady, Zaruna of the Night ... Secret God-

dess – thy servants call upon thee, for this is the time of the festival. Come now and honour our circle. Enter, Maiden, come now to thy throne and bless thy servants. Come. Come, come…

Later the High Priestess says:

This is the festival of womankind and the night of the Goddess whom we worship, the Lady, the Moon, Zaruna. Yet the Goddess alone is without her consort and her presence here does not mean that the God is no more. The men folk are without on this night. How say you, servants of Zaruna, shall we let them enter?

The assembled women then decide whether the men should be allowed to join the circle. In practice they always decide in favour but if for some reason the men are vetoed for the night, then it is up to the High Priestess to deal with any other magic and formally close the ceremony.

THE SPRING EQUINOX

The ceremony of the spring equinox calls for flowers and greenery decorating the altar. The purpose behind the ritual is to entreat the Lady to bless new born animals and crops. The High Priestess blesses unsown seed. The wine is blessed and that which is not drunk is poured on the fields. Today the bonfire is likely to be a token one, i.e. a special candle, and the wine is likely to be poured on the front garden. Leaping dances are out of the question in most flats but the rejoicing ceremony remains the same.

THE SPRING INVOCATION

Hear ye servants of our Lady Queen Zaruna and know that this is the time that the goddess is renewed in all her glory. She is beauteous and young once more. Tall and graceful she walks among us as a maiden and our beloved one. Come, our fairest lady. Grant blessing unto the seeds which become the flowers of tomorrow. Come

O gracious lady and protect that which is newly born, that children and animals may grow strong beneath thy hands. Let the seed be blessed in Thy Name, O Zaruna. Let the wine be blessed which is the wine of spring and the wine of the Queen.
Let the seed be cast to the earth. Let the fire of joy be lit and let the wine be shared.

The men of the coven take the seed from the High Priestess and throw it outside the circle. The High Priestess blesses the wine and her women pass it around the circle. The High Priest lights the 'bonfire' which is a signal for the party to begin.

MAY EVE

This isn't really a working ceremony at all – it is a celebration of the fact that the Goddess and the God are lovers who bring forth the new crops and so on. Ideally it requires a site with a may-pole, a marvellous party laid on and an all-night session in the woods. In practice the High Priest represents the God and he moves about the circle seeking for the Goddess. When the High Priestess is found, she is dressed with flowers, ribbons and perfume for the Goddess was the original May Queen.

The High Priest says, *I bless the crops and the animals. I bless the seeds and the roots. I bless the stems and the buds. I bless the coming of life in plants, in animals and in children in the Name of Zarach.*

The High Priestess says, *I bless the new growth and the new born, I bless the seeds and the roots. I bless the stems and the buds. I bless the coming of life in plants, in animals and in children in the Name of Zaruna.*

They turn to each other and say together, *God and Goddess, Blessed be.*

And the party lasts for the rest of the evening.

THE SUMMER SOLSTICE

The cauldron is placed before the altar. It is filled with

water and decorated with summer flowers. Coven members stand around the circle, men and women alternately. The High Priest stands in the North and the High Priestess faces him in the South where she invokes the sun:

Lord of Heaven and Power of the Sun, We invoke thee in the secret name of Zarach, O Lord of Greatest Light. Now is the time of your glory and power. Place your shield between us and all power of darkness. Shoot forth your arrows of light to protect us. Grant to us at this time green fields and good hunting. Give to us orchards of fullness and corn that has risen high. Show us within the time of Splendour the pathway to the place of the Lord and the Lady.

The High Priestess draws a pentacle above the altar. She plunges the tip of her wand into the cauldron, withdraws it and holds it upright, saying, *The knife to the cup, the rod to the cauldron, the sun to the earth but the flesh to the spirit.*

The High Priest then salutes the High Priestess and speaks words of ancient wisdom as follows:

Now is the time of the sun in its glory when our Lord Zarach is at his height in the heavens. Yet it must also be remembered that now also is the time of Zarach's decline to his death and rebirth at the darkest time of winter. As it is with the God, so it is with man. We also journey throughout our time, from birth unto death and to rebirth upon our way. We must remember that the goddess Zaruna will raise the God with the kiss of rebirth and send him yet again upon his journey. We also go down into the cloak of Zaruna's darkness and her veils hide us from mortal sight. But the tomb is the womb of time from which we return to other lives, to share once more the knowledge and love of our fellows and our friends.

The High Priestess then says, *Dance, one and all, dance about the cauldron of the Craft. Be blessed by the waters of Zaruna that are contained in the cauldron, and remember that which you have heard this night.*

The coven dance three times around the circle while the High Priestess sprinkles them all with water. This is followed by initiations, cakes and wine, etc.

AUGUST EVE

The Lammas eve ceremony is the converse of the Candlemas one. The men proceed to the circle and set it up on their own. The High Priest invokes the God and any exclusively masculine magic gets done at this stage. The men are then reminded of the fact that the coven women are waiting and may – or may not – be invited in for the occasion. If the women are permitted to enter, they will be taught some secret of hunting magic and reminded that the God's death is, in itself, a promise of rebirth.

Lammas invocation (done by the High Priest):

Lord of the Sun, the Hunt and the Fire, Zarach, be with us now before the time of departure. We call upon thee this night for this is the time of thy festival. Come unto us, we beg and honour our circle. Come, before the time of departure is upon us, come and bless this rite.

Later the High Priest says:

This is the festival of man, the hunt and the harvest which provides for the time of darkness. Yet the God stands alone without his proper consort. She must grieve for his departure and take him to the dark places. The women folk have been excluded on this night. How say you, servants of Zarach, shall we let them enter?

If it is decided against the women entering, the men must complete the ceremony and close the ritual of their own accord but this very seldom happens.

It is far more likely that the women will be called to witness that the God Zarach is now dying, but even in his death he gives strength to the grain, life to the harvest and so on. Initiations can be held, cakes and wine will be shared before the festival ends.

The altar is decorated with autumn leaves, ears of corn, pine cones and so on. The ceremony serves a double purpose, first to thank the Lord and Lady for their bounty, much as a harvest festival. However, because it is Autumn, the Lord is barely present and the feast is also our hope for his rebirth. The High Priest stands West of the altar and the High Priestess in the East.

High Priest: *We are met at this time to give thanks to the God and the Goddess for that which we have received throughout the year. We have harvested their gifts and stored away the food for the time of darkness is upon us. I ask and implore that Zarach shall bless the seed corn that is ours for the coming year for, although the god is in darkness, we will remember that he will come again.*

High Priestess: *Zarach, we call upon you, our hidden god who goes through the realm of death to gain life and rebirth and youth. Zarach our God and Zaruna our queen, accept our thanks for the gifts which you have given us in this year. Preserve us in the dark days when food is scarce. Keep from us the threat of famine. Give us hope through the night for Zarach has gone to the place of death. Mother-Goddess, Zaruna, Dark Queen – grant to him rebirth. Zaruna, dread queen, let Zarach return to us, his people. Zaruna, death goddess, in you is all the future. Goddess most gentle – let the fire be lit to celebrate our faith in the return.*

(The High Priest salutes the High Priestess who lights the fire. She holds her rod to the skies and says:)

The Goddess hears. Zaruna answers. The wheel of night and day spins on and the Lord will return to us. Let this bring rejoicing.

(The High Priestess leads the dancing. Initiations follow, cakes and wine or any other business before the party ends.)

SAMHAIN OR HALLOWE'EN

Hallowe'en is a joyful ceremony and marks the end and the beginning of the Craft year. Ideally one should proceed to the ritual dancing the whole way, riding a broomstick and carrying a torch. Whatever the customs of the past, the ceremony today is more frequently held indoors. Orange candles are used, though occasionally black ones are put out because they are in keeping with 'the feast of the living and the dead'. Like other ceremonies, this one starts with a prayer of protection against unbelievers. There is a 'Call to the Dead' that those who were of the coven, those who are and those who will be of the coven shall join the meeting. There is a brief silence before the Moon Goddess is invoked. A cup of wine is blessed in the name of the Dark Mother and those whom she governs. The meeting is then open for a general discussion on future policy. Initiations may be held and feasting follows, with dancing.

According to one school of thought it is considered discourteous to dismiss the dead guests. In practice a 'Farewell' is often given just before dawn and the wine is poured on the ground as the candles are extinguished.

The prayer for protection is quoted elsewhere.

CALL TO THE DEAD

'Harken to the voice of our souls and hear us, ye who wander. Harken for we call upon those who have passed from this life, back through the generations of man to the time of our first parents. We light the beacon that you are guided to this place and we call upon you. Listen to the voices of our souls, all those of the past. Harken to us, those who shall be of our house. The gulf between the worlds is narrow at this time. Approach all those who were of the Craft. Come, those who are of the Craft. Come, those who will be of the Craft, come and share our joy this night. Let the cup be filled in the name of the three, for we would speak once more to those who have passed from us and we will see those who are yet to be. Come to us and rejoice.'

INVOCATION TO THE MOON

'Zaruna, Queen of the midnight skies, we rejoice in thy blessing. We call upon thy maiden beauty to bless us with insight and serenity. We invoke thy silver graciousness to light the ways of lovers and guard the sleep of children. We call upon thy dark aspect this night, the lady of the dead and the unborn, cast back thy cloak and grant us sight of these. Show us in this darkness thine understanding and grant, Zaruna, blessing.'

BLESSING OF THE WINE

'Zaruna, Dark Queen, bless the wine in this cup in token of the cauldron which contained three drops of wisdom for all the world. Creatures of earth and creatures of water, creatures of air and creatures of fire, friends in life and friends in death! Gather here in the dark Queen's name, that ere she gathers earth unto her again.'

DANCE

Power of stone and power of earth,
Power that shapes our place of birth,
Spin the wheel of night and day
Spin the wheel OR-AH-AY

Power of ice and water free,

Power that hides the depth of sea,
Weave the web of night and day,
Spin the wheel OR-AH-AY

Power of wind and power of air,

Power of mountains bleak and bare,
Turn the time of night and day,
Spin the wheel OR-AH-AY

Power of flame and power of fire,
Power of all our vast desire,
Light of dark and light of day,
Spin the wheel OR-AH-AY

THE FAREWELL BEFORE DAWN

'Friends of today, friends of yesteryear and friends that are yet to be, we have met and rejoiced this night in our knowledge that time is no barrier and that friendship endures. Yet the hours of our feast draw to their close and time brings this feast to its end. Therefore go to your appointed places disturbing not those who would fear you, nor harming any substance of this world. Remember that we will meet again some other Hallows Eve. So let it end with love and blessing on us all.'

YULE – THE WINTER SOLSTICE

The cauldron of the Craft is placed in the centre of the circle. It should be placed over a fire of wood gathered by all members of the coven. The wood represents all that was evil, dark and old and all that one would like to be rid of. In due course it will be destroyed by fire. The lights are extinguished and the fire is lit. From the fire, candles are lit and those within the circle begin the dance which denotes the strengthening of light and life from the darkest time of the year. In practice few yule ceremonies are ever worked out of doors. Very often the cauldron contains the bits and pieces for the fire, instead of boiling over it. The occasion is one of rejoicing, followed by a feast.

INCANTATION

Queen of Heaven, moon and night,
Water, air and fire and earth,
Widowed queen, return the One
Bring the light unto its birth.
Queen of sadness, grieving woe,
Queen of future, queen of bane,
Queen that guards the new and past,
Grant that light return again.
Rise, O Child and new beginning,
Show thy light to all the world.
Light above the land and ocean,

Be the veil of darkness furled.
Blessed is the triple mother,
Queen of Dark and Queen of Day,
Hers the dance and hers rejoicing,
AP – AP – AN – O – IR – Ut-AY

This invocation is followed by initiations, if any, and cakes and wine, etc.

THE FIRST INITIATION

The circle is set up with everything in its proper place. Prayers for protection are made and any secret business that the candidate is not permitted to see, is dealt with, for the candidate is not in the room. If the ceremony is held out of doors, then the candidate must be far enough away to neither see nor hear what is happening. The circle is opened by placing two lighted white candles in the West. These mark the 'gateway'. The High Priestess spreads out her hands over the circle at this point and delegates a messenger to bring the candidate to the edge of the circle. The messenger returns to his place, leaving the candidate to face the High Priestess or Priest. The candidate is outside the circle, the priestess inside.
Priestess Seeker, you have moved through life unto this place. Know that if you come within this circle, you have departed from the world of men. You have heard tell of dread domains and strange perils, of terrible fates and awesome beings. Know that there is time to turn back. You may go from this place without one word of reproach, no blame, no loss of courage. Will you go back now?
Candidate I will not go back.*
Priestess Then come within the circle of your own free will, no one assisting you in any way. Stand where I shall indicate (the West side of the altar). Be the God and Goddess the witnesses that you have entered this place

* If the candidate decides against joining the Craft at this point, he is free to go and you never discuss his reasons for going or mention the Craft.

of your own will, fairly warned beforehand of that which might follow.

Candidate I seek the path of the Wise, the secret learning before the sign of the Craft.

High Priestess The secret learning is not lightly given, yet, with study, it is yours. The sign of the Craft is the sign of the Pentagram. Know that this is our shield against the outside world. The Pentagram is also the sign of the star which we follow. The Pentagram is that on which we swear an oath unto the Craft.

Candidate I would swear that oath.

High Priestess Think before you swear, for the oath of the Craft is not an easy promise to stand by. It has brought to those bound by it pain and suffering in the past. It has brought torture and death to many who were only suspected of practising its mysteries. Remember the burning time when all we could promise our associates was a painless death before the flames took hold. Do you still desire to take that oath, knowing that what has been may yet be again?

Candidate I will take the oath.

High Priestess Put your right hand upon this symbol and your left hand in mine. Now say after me:

> Before the Lord and the Lady, I . . . do of my own will, most solemnly swear to keep secret the knowledge of the Craft which shall be given to me. I swear before the God and the Goddess that I will not betray my associates in the Craft, however greatly I am tempted or tortured to do so. I swear before the Lord and the Lady that I will not use the knowledge I am given in any evil manner to cause trouble to my fellow men. I will hold my knowledge secret still, save to my associates of the Craft. This I do swear before Zarach and Zaruna. So be it.

High Priestess (Touching the candidate's forehead and hands with charged oil) With oil I consecrate you priest and witch. (Touching same with water) With water I consecrate you priest and witch. (Picking up a candle and moving it through the sign of the Pentagram.) With fire I consecrate you priest and witch.

All New made witch, I salute you.

High Priestess It is our tradition that in this hour you choose a new name by which your associates shall know you. Many have chosen the names of great practitioners who have gone from hence but this is by no means essential. Speak now your new name.

Candidate My new name is . . .

(The High Priestess repeats the name and everyone else repeats it after her.)

High Priestess Candidates, the gifts of the Lord and the Lady are multitudinous blessings and in token of this, we will give you a gift in this hour. Receive, therefore, this Athame, which we have made in our circle. This is the weapon of a witch and, using this, you shall fashion things considered by the ignorant to be magic. Keep this weapon with you at all times. Let none other touch it lest they harm your own being. With this Athame you are as you are made this night, priest and witch.

Use your Athame to cut and fashion your own wand of magic to your desire, for this is yours to do and none may aid you in the task.

Use your Athame to engrave the sign of the Pentacle for this shall be a shield against rebellious spirits.

You are familiar with the other tools unto the altar of the Craft. You see the Cup of the Goddess, the burning incense and the candles which light our pathway. Take now the witch cord which I give to you and wear it as a new insignia. Stand where I shall indicate (in front of the altar).

Mighty Ones of the World above, know that . . . is a priest and witch before Zarach and Zaruna.

Mighty Ones of the Worlds below, know that . . . is a priest and witch before Zarach and Zaruna.

Mighty ones of the Eastern Quarter, know that . . . is a priest and witch before Zarach and Zaruna.

Mighty Ones of the Southern Quarter, know that . . . is a priest and witch before Zarach and Zaruna.

Mighty Ones of the Western Quarter, know that . . . is a priest and witch before Zarach and Zaruna.

Mighty Ones of the Northern Quarter, know that . . . is a priest and witch before Zarach and Zaruna.

. . . before Zarach and Zaruna, I salute thee.

This is one form of Craft initiation. It is fair to say that there are other forms. Some of them call for a purification by scourging. Some call for intercourse. Undoubtedly some of the 'initiations' we have come across have been physically harmful to the candidates themselves for the scourging has marked them all the days of their lives. Some of these so-called rituals have provided a new line in pornography, complete with 'blue films' afterwards.

Many covens insist that the candidate should be ritually bound and barely be able to hobble into the Circle. Others prefer the candidate to be bound before the scourging takes place. The more responsible Craft covens seem to feel that a candidate must enter freely and that joining must be the candidate's choice and being led in by the end of a rope with ankles bound is the wrong thing to do.

Never join a coven on impulse – think carefully. Ask if nudity, scourging, or intercourse are a part of their working. Nudity is debated in Witchcraft circles and used by a minority of Craft members. Scourging should not be used, it causes grievous bodily harm and on occasions the 'witches' who use scourging have vanished into the night with a crop of interesting pictures and left a totally bewildered candidate behind. Craft members loathe this sort of thing because it stirs up public opinion against the sincere Craft members. Ritual intercourse is left to individual Coven members to decide on – it does NOT turn up in a first initiation ceremony. Do not join the 'coven' that insists that it does. Remember, never join on impulse. Take time and think about it carefully.

INITIATION – SECOND DEGREE *

The circle is set up and the altar prepared. When all is ready, the High Priestess turns to the candidate

High Priestess Stand where I shall indicate (before the altar).

Mighty Ones of the World above, know that . . . is now prepared to be made a High Priest of Zarach and Zaruna.

Mighty Ones of the World below, know that . . . is now prepared to be made a High Priest of Zarach and Zaruna.

Mighty Ones of the Eastern Quarter, know that . . . is now prepared to be made a High Priest of Zarach and Zaruna.

Mighty Ones of the Southern Quarter, know that . . . is now prepared to be made a High Priest of Zarach and Zaruna.

Mighty Ones of the Western Quarter, know that . . . is now prepared to be made a High Priest of Zarach and Zaruna.

Mighty Ones of the Northern Quarter, know that . . . is now prepared to be made a High Priest of Zarach and Zaruna.

. . . Speak now, before the God and the Goddess who weigh your most secret heart. State first what you have done with your knowledge.

Candidate I have guarded my knowledge from the profane who would dishonour that knowledge. I have sought to further my own studies with the help of my fellow Craft members. I have kept secret the rituals and ceremonies of the God and the Goddess, nor have I spoken their secret names to any man. I have kept faith with my fellow Craft members and betrayed them not to their enemies. This I swore to do and all this have I done.

* Not all covens recognize three degrees – some work their own promotions based on different theories and give other titles!

High Priestess What do you seek within this next degree?
Candidate I seek to better serve the Lord and the Lady.
High Priestess It is said that the Craft is a way of power, yet before power is given, there is an oath to be sworn.
Candidate I can but swear that which I have sworn before, not to betray my secrets, nor my associates. I honour the God Zarach and the Goddess Zaruna and this I will swear, that I serve them as Lord and as Lady. They will see into my soul and know of truth. They will weigh my heart against any oath. If I am faithful to them, the Lord and the Lady shall be my reward. If I am faithless, then the years are long before I shall find them out again. If I am too daring, then Zarach and Zaruna will turn from me and in this moment destroy me.
High Priestess You have called destruction if you are unworthy of this degree. The God and the Goddess are your judge. (Pause.) Destruction is with-held. Therefore do I consecrate you with the earth at your feet, for you are and shall remain a child of the earth though you follow the God and the Goddess.

I consecrate you with water, that it shall symbolize all your desire in the time to come.

I consecrate you with air, that it shall be your will to worship Zarach and Zaruna unto all your days.

I consecrate you with fire, that you shall be a light to your fellow Craft members for all of their days, working as a High Priest before Zarach and Zaruna. Be the God and the Goddess my witness in this hour that . . . shall be a High Priest before ye.

(The High Priestess turns to the altar and rests her hands upon it, invoking all her strength and blessing from the Goddess. After a pause she turns, places her hands on the shoulders of the Candidate and says): Unto Thee be the power. This do I will.
Candidate Let blessing be.
High Priestess I consecrate thee by the earth upon which your feet go.

I consecrate thee by the water which is love and secret knowledge.

I consecrate thee by the air which is a will to magical power.

I consecrate thee by the fire which cleanses all things.

Above that which is below do I consecrate thee.

Below that which is above do I consecrate thee, High Priest and Witch before the Lord and the Lady.

(Some covens insist that the candidate now scourges the High Priestess at this point. After that, one of the traditional Craft legends is acted out. Sometimes this is the story of the goddess seeking out the God through the Underworld. Sometimes it is a more modern story of Craft history with the emphasis on the Craft in the World of today. An ancient story will involve an official Narrator and coven members mime their parts with the newly-made High Priest also taking a part in the story. A modern story, i.e. the story of the witches who stopped Adolph Hitler just before Dunkirk, will probably be narration only. Done properly in the right atmosphere, it is a very telling experience. The Narrator finishes with the words, 'For this is a tale of our people and now it is ended.'

Candidate You have told a tale of yesterday, yet we have still to weave the tales of tomorrow. For tomorrow is mist and moonlight only. It is a tale with less substance than dreams and tomorrow is hidden away within the Goddess. It is we who shall make it real.

High Priestess Hear ye, Dwellers in the World above and know that . . . is a consecrated High Priest before the God and the Goddess.

Hear ye, Dwellers in the World below and know that . . . is a consecrated High Priest before the God and the Goddess.

Hear ye, Dwellers in the Eastern Quarter and know that . . . is a consecrated High Priest before the God and the Goddess.

Hear ye, Dwellers in the Southern Quarter and know that . . . is a consecrated High Priest before the God and the Goddess.

Hear ye, Dwellers in the Western Quarter and know that . . . is a consecrated High Priest before the God and the Goddess.

Hear ye, Dwellers in the Northern Quarter and know that . . . is a consecrated High Priest before the God and the Goddess.

Let blessing be.

THE THIRD DEGREE OR SO-CALLED 'GREAT RITE'

There is a lot of misunderstanding about this particular ritual. If you believe the newspapers or the writers of occult fiction, you might be forgiven for assuming that this is the 'Black Mass' and it's all very weird. Nonetheless the Great Rite is probably the oldest of all magical rituals, common to mankind the world over. Even today it is used – and at times abused – by Craft members, magicians of all types and varieties and plenty of other people in the 'occult world'.

The idea behind the Great Rite is that of asking the God and the Goddess to aid in the conception of a leader of men, it might be a tribal king or the next High Priest or some special soul. Obviously the conception of the next hero was far too important to be left to chance for such a hero could lead the coven to the Happy Lands where game was plentiful, the land ran rivers of wine and no man oppressed any other, or whatever particular sort of heaven you needed. The mother of such a hero was chosen with care. The child was conceived with all your best magic. Sometimes the High Priest played the part of the God. Sometimes the Priestess took the part of the Goddess but either way the child conceived was regarded as a very special entity. Where the Craft was concerned, the magical child was the responsibility of the coven who were bound to support the child and the mother to their utmost ability. Born into the Craft, the child had no need of initiations or tests. He stood in a special position as a super-human who, in childhood, must be cared for and defended against evil, if necessary with the lives of other coven members.

Used in its original form, the ritual is primitive but it is effective. Obviously much depends on what sort of a child you ask for – asking for a child who will lead the children of men to a peaceful world is surely a laudable intention.

The ritual described above is often referred to as The Rite of Tanith. It is confused with 'The Black Mass' though it has NOTHING to do with the Black Mass which is simply the ordinary Mass read backwards and shouldn't have a girl on the altar anyway!

The Great Rite is also confused with 'The Mass of Saint Secairie', this is a ceremony purporting to involve magical intercourse between a priest and a woman to cause trouble or death. The stories of this ceremony appear to originate in the late Middle Ages. I have been unable to trace an authentic ritual by this name but one must take into account the environment of the Middle Ages, a time of superstition and a time when various members of the priesthood were well hated as money grubbers whose celibacy was debatable. Undoubtedly those within the monasteries were better off than most of the peasants but physically healthy men in a monastery were open to temptation. Under such circumstances the priest might well take his mistress to a desolate place but probably more for a biological need rather than a dirty magical deed! Nevertheless the legend grew up and the whisper that 'he has been seen working the Mass of St Secairie' was enough to cause fair trouble.

Occult fiction writers have combined factors from all three ceremonies in books that deal with witches and black magicians. This has confused the general public and not surprisingly. To add to the confusion, occult fiction writers insist that this sort of thing must be done in the ruins of a desecrated church with the climax occuring on the stroke of midnight.

But consider the early Christians. St Augustine was advised to build Christian churches on pagan holy spots and amalgamate the pagan gods with Christian saints. Not surprisingly the pagans still regarded the holy spots as their own though there was a new temple to a stranger god within the holy wood or on top of the sacred hill. It would cause no end of trouble to be found in your own holy place during the day so when could you use the ancient spot without detection? Obviously in the middle of the night! So long as the pagans were home by cock-crow, no one would be any the wiser and the ancient gods would still be happy with their worshippers. If the church had fallen into disuse, so much the better for there would be less chance of interruption by a sleepy and furious priest. One must allow for the fact that the pagans had a point of view – even if one does not share that viewpoint.

However, just occasionally the secret gatherings of the Craft and other groups did get overlooked by outsiders. Non-initiates are not the best people to describe what is going on in any magical ceremony. They would neither see what was going on clearly, nor would they hear it all and they would probably be scared stiff at the thought of what these folks would do if discovered in their secret rites. Consequently some of the reporting is highly suspect to say the very least. Small wonder that the Craft have a name for wholesale orgies and so on.

To be absolutely fair, this country escaped most of the Witchcraft persecutions. For a very great deal of our history the penalty for practising witchcraft was six hours in the stocks and/or a year in prison. The death penalty was given when high treason was suspected or when death by poison was involved. Treason meant death by fire but the poison penalty was a different matter. Poison was something that not many people understood. Some of the symptoms were known but proving poison without today's forensic science was a problem. No one could say with certainty what the poison was. Nobody could say with certainty who had prepared the poison which is not the same thing as who administered it. Poison was supposed to be something the witches knew about and, to be fair, the Craft members probably knew more about plants, herbs and toxic vegetation than anyone else. The death penalty for poisoning was understandable in the circumstances and it follows the original Biblical command, 'Thou shalt not suffer a dealer in poisons to live.'

But the witches today are not blamed usually for poison, they are blamed for orgies, 'the Black Mass' and so on. Here for the first time is the Witches Great Rite written out in full.

The Coven assembles and the circle is prepared. The prayer for protection is chanted and the circle is worked. Cakes and wine are given. Then everyone who is not sufficiently advanced in the Craft is sent away. The altar is moved out of the circle if necessary.

The High Priestess then addresses the man and the woman, reminding them that this must be their own choice. If they elect proper intercourse before the Powers, then it must be a wholehearted committal for a magical child, not just a private party under rather unusual conditions. The decision is left entirely to the two people involved and, with these words, the High Priestess departs. Every one else who has remained goes with her, leaving the couple to themselves.

Left alone together, the woman gives the man the ancient five-fold salute and, possibly, a ritual scourging. He returns the same. The man then 'Draws down the Moon' on the woman's body. In theory they then decide whether to do the Great Rite completely or token only.

The decision having been taken, the woman then lies down in the centre of the circle with her head towards the North. The man stands at her feet.

Woman I am she who is called Zaruna by men who desire me. That which I represent is yours for I give pleasure and love most freely. Only be pure of heart and body and soul if you would know that which I am.

Man I am desirous of your gifts and I come to honour you. Seeking the love of the Goddess I come to receive your gifts.

Woman In this moment, come.

(The man goes down to her and covers her body with his own. If the intercourse is a token one only, that is all that happens. Otherwise they both lie perfectly still so as not to excite each other. It is essential to come to the end of the following speech before orgasm is reached.)

Woman I am the joy of the earth but unto my children I am also the ecstasy of the spirit. Mine is the Law of Love, for I am Joy in the heart of a man. I am the Goddess of all Life and my Love moves throughout existence. I am all Beauty. I am all Desire. I am beloved of the God and all mankind. I am she whom you seek in this hour and yet I was with you before the dawn of time and I shall enfold you at time's ending. I am the end of all desire. Let blessing be.

Man Let blessing be.

After a short interval, the Great Rite being over, the two celebrants of the Great Rite rise in silence. The senior of the pair ends the ceremony and closes the Circle, putting out candles and so on. They then robe and join the others.

Later that evening there may be some form of presentation, a snakeskin garter for the girl, possibly a magical sword for the man.

The 'Great Rite' is not used by every witch coven, indeed many covens would throw up their hands in horror at the thought of it! Other covens, intent on staying within the morals of the land, allow this only between married couples. Other covens again insist that the private life of witches and outsiders belongs in the bedroom and not in a magic circle at all. Contrary to the Sunday newspapers, opinion on this ceremony is deeply divided within the Craft.

It is to be hoped that this book will clear up some of the misunderstandings and bring more tolerance between the Craft and the outside world. If so, I have not dared a coven's death curse in vain.